TOYOTA
Illustrated Encyclopedia of Lean Management

Kaizen, 5S System,
Total Quality Management, Just In Time,
Pull System, Poka-Yoke, Kanban,
Muda, Mura, Muri, Jidoka, Gemba...

An Internationally Proven
Practical Step by Step
Training Manual
For Creating a Culture of Powerful
Proactive Organizational Effectiveness,
Business Success and Sustainability

Also available with
Large Poster Prints
and
Organizational Training and Development Program

Gabriel Iqbal, BSc (Hons) PGCE (Science Education), University of Leeds, UK

TOYOTA
Illustrated Encyclopedia of Lean Management

Kaizen, 5S System,
Total Quality Management, Just In Time,
Pull System, Poka-Yoke, Kanban,
Muda, Mura, Muri, Jidoka, Gemba…

An Internationally Proven Practical Step by Step
Training Manual For Creating a Culture of
Powerful Proactive Organizational Effectiveness,
Business Success and Sustainability

ASIN: B019UGXI94
ISBN-13: 978-1519412898
ISBN-10: 1519412894

Category: Organizational Development - Leadership - Business - Sustainability

Published under licence by Eureka Academy - Canada
Tel: +1 647 782 1115   Fax: +1 905 257 8077
email: eureka.academy@eurekamakingadifference.com

w w w . e u r e k a m a k i n g a d i f f e r e n c e . c o m

Also see the masterpiece work by the author on:

w w w . h e a r t i n t e l l i g e n c e b o o k . c o m

CONTENTS

UNDERSTANDING AND APPLYING LEAN MANAGEMENT - AN ENCYCLOPEDIC APPROACH 72

Heart Intelligence Film Documentary

Available for viewing at no cost on the official website of
Heart Intelligence – Book Trilogy

Processes can become unproductive and time is wasted when one process waits to begin while another ends.

The emphasis on the **Pull** and **Single Flow** shows how operations can be smooth, uninterrupted and continuous.

A poignant fact that is elucidated is that estimates suggest that as much as **99 percent** of a product's time in manufacture is actually spent **"waiting"**.

ACKNOWLEDGEMENTS

To my family and friends,
for your love and encouragement.

To my wife Tracy Liu for her spirited companionship and to our daughters Rumi and Roya
for bringing out the best in us.

To my parents and Tracy's parents for their
support and warmth.

REVIEWS

area will be invaluable in preparing
students to steward the world
of the future." "Gabriel leads by
example and has successfully
started the first active recycling
program at the school."
"Gabriel has an unrelenting passion
for teaching science that comes
out when you talk to him.
Some people are good at what
they do- some love what they do –
Gabriel has both."

- Chisholm Academy, Canada

-

"Gabriel has bought a lot
of fresh lateral thinking
and out of the box solutions."
"His involvement and enthusiasm
is commendable and a breath
of fresh air in our organization."

- Kempinski Hotels, 5 Star Resorts, Switzerland

-

"Gabriel is very passionate
about sustainability and has
involved our entire team into
effective resource conservation."

- ReMax Real Estate, Canada

-

"Gabriel has uncovered the mechanics
of the flow of creativity within
each of us and between each of
our team members.
Gabriel's genuine follow-ups and
individual consultation with our
team members makes his
contributions both unique and
very appreciable. We recommend
Gabriel's services to all who
seek continued development and
a vision to prosper in a well-balanced culture."

- Novell, USA

-

"Gabriel Makes The Difference."
"Gabriel walks the talk."
"This is a timely message."

- Peel Multicultural Council, Canada

-

"Gabriel is a joy to work with
and as a leader inspires the team
in an unconventional
yet powerful manner.
He played a key role in
the improvement of quality.
Gabriel has always amazed us as
a human being as someone
who comes across
very different from the crowd."

- Tyco International, USA

-

"Gabriel shows an exceptional interest
in biological study and produces
above standard, accurate
and well expressed work."

**- Ealing, Hammersmith and
West London College, UK**

-

"Gabriel is a committed and pragmatic business professional and brings about the best of dedicated team dynamics and planning of organizational structure within the administrative systems of his corporate clients." "Gabriel is passionate about what he refers to as Information Age Team Dynamics that are far advanced then the Industrial Age organizational systems."

- BTL Worldwide, Dubai

-

"Amazing, we have learnt so much."

- George Brown College, Canada

-

ABOUT THE AUTHOR

Gabriel Iqbal, is an award-winning internationally acclaimed Canadian lean management, leadership, behavioural skills and sustainability training specialist. He is a paradigm shifting scientist, author, poet and humanitarian.

After having secured a scholarship for distinguished performance in a Diploma in Health Sciences at Ealing, Hammersmith and West London College, UK, in the early 90's, he was privileged to work under one of the world's eminent Biologist, Dr. Ray McNeil Alexander and earned a BSc. Honours in Biology from the University of Leeds, UK, with a key focus on Biomechanics, Fresh Water Ecology, Environmental Science, Evolution, Paleobiology, and Human Psychology. Later on he completed a Post-Graduation in Science Education from the same university and taught Science for several years. Further, his career focused on Lean Management, Sustainable Development, Organizational Behaviour, and Wellbeing. He has worked internationally for almost 25 years, with various fortune 500 companies, written extensively on Lean Management, Sustainable Development and Behavioural Skills and implemented his signature programs at the grassroots level with practical success.

Gabriel is also a Lean Management Certified Trainer and a Certified Internal Auditor for Environmental Health and Safety Management Systems that includes ISO 14001 (Environmental Management Systems Training) and OHSAS 18001 (Occupational Health and Safety Management Systems Training). Following his professional education his personal interests grew in the field of Behavioural Psychology, Human Motivation and Sustainable Development. Gabriel has provided Ethical Leadership, Management, Corporate and Social Responsibility, Human Motivation, Sustainable Development and Well-being Programs for over two decades via his training and development organization, the Eureka Academy. Gabriel's major work is represented in, *"Heart Intelligence"* – Book Trilogy, which is accompanied by a non-profit Film:

www.heartintelligencebook.com

Gabriel has authored various books that are available on Amazon:

www.amazon.com/Gabriel-Iqbal/e/B00PTJ0OIK

He has written extensively on the subjects of Lean Management, Leadership, Environmental Sustainability and Well-being. To find out more, please visit the Eureka Academy website:

www.eurekamakingadifference.com

For his international works and services Gabriel has received the following awards:

- **Making a Difference Award 2011**
  Peel Multicultural Council, Canada

- **Outstanding Guest Speaker Award 2010**
  International Leadership Congress

- **International e-learning Award 2011**
  International e-learning Congress

Gabriel is married to Tracy Liu and they have two daughters, Rumi and Roya and live in Oakville, Ontario, Canada.

EUREKA ACADEMY TRAINING

This encyclopedia was initially written in 2011, as manual by the author for building up the knowledge pool at Eureka Academy, Canada. The purpose was to fill in our internationally growing training demand from various multinational organizations, schools, colleges, universities including government institutions. The applications of this encyclopedia for proactive organizational effectiveness and sustainability are proven across a diverse spectrum of organizations as it is simple, basic and fundamentally a rigorous disciplinary methodology that produces practical organizational effectiveness and sustainable results.

WHO ARE WE ?

Eureka Academy offers an International Award-Winning Service with 25 Years of Global Workforce Development Experience in Multiple Fortune 500 Companies.

WHAT DO WE DO ?

We have got a Great Reason for creating Motivated and Responsible Brand Ambassadors. It's called "Self Development".

HOW DO WE DO IT ?

We instill: Trust   Inter-dependence   Win-Win Strategies   Proactive Consciousness

OUR GOAL

Our aim is to inspire, educate and empower people and businesses to appreciably increase their performance while imparting a balanced approach for consistently improving the quality of their lives and the lives of those around them.

Our goal is to work collectively as part of a world community and re-engineer Scientific Ethics and Principles for the betterment of the Global Human Condition and a Sustainable Future that works in Harmony with the Balanced Phenomena of Natural Law.

"Our Mission is to
Make a Difference
by
Balancing
Peak Performance
and
Sustainability."

Eureka Academy, Canada

PREVIEW

This encyclopedia is an Internationally Proven Practical Step by Step Training Manual For Creating a Culture of Powerful Proactive Organizational Effectiveness, Business Success and Sustainability.

Paradigm shifting scientist, author and lean management specialist, Gabriel Iqbal has created a practical ready reference on "HOW TO" engage Lean Management as opposed to "WHAT IS" Lean Management.

This is an authoritative and simple step by step training manual explaining the TPS (Toyota Production System). Toyota's world-class Lean Management System is fully described here in animated form for people to learn and apply in any area where efficiency and effectiveness holds top priority. This encyclopedia belongs in the collection of any person who seeks success in business, professional development, self-development and sustainable development.

This illustrated encyclopedia is designed with large fonts, templates, bullet pointed flowcharts, diagrams, graphics that can all be used as a plug and play visual experience.

The encyclopedia demonstrates how Toyota developed their systematic process, human potential, ingenuity and rigorous discipline. Their adventure and the development of the Management Principles that support any quest of world class processes management and world class quality is communicated via a fully comprehensive and animated encyclopedic form.

The Toyota management principles apply to any business and in any industry, including distribution, software development, manufacturing, hospitals and healthcare, government, education, retail, hospitality, anything and everything that involves processes management and human development will benefit from the principles and practices of this encyclopedia.

This encyclopedia is very powerful in setting up a proactive culture shift in any organization. If you are not into organizational development and are happy with status quo, then don't read this encyclopedia. It is guaranteed that after reading this encyclopedia you will either become an outcast, a maverick, or will start your own business. You will stick out in the band and see nothing but "Lean Management". The most rewarding virtue you will develop from this revolutionary encyclopedia is that you will generate a consistently disciplined energizing habit of effectiveness and proactive solution oriented efficiency.

The author describes how processes can become unproductive and time is wasted when one process waits to begin while another ends. The emphasis on the Pull and Single Flow shows how operations can be smooth, uninterrupted and continuous. A poignant fact that is elucidated is that estimates suggest that as much as 99 percent of a product's time in manufacture is actually spent "waiting". (International Journal of Emerging Technology and Advanced Engineering Certified Journal, Volume 3, Issue 11, November 2013)

The chapter on The Zen of Lean is a real treat, as it gives you an energizing, vivid and transcendental perspective behind what the author believes as the metaphysical dimensions of the subject.

It is a must read, especially for anyone in corporate America where the technology curve and work culture, have been for the past few decades on the overall decline.

Make sure to write your name on this encyclopedia as it has the habit of being passed on from person to person – and before you know it, the effectiveness becomes contagious !

INTRODUCTION

"If I really want to improve my situation,
I can work on the one thing over which I have control - myself."

Stephen R. Covey, The 7 Habits of Highly Effective People

In a fast changing world that is continuously and rapidly changing, Toyota has managed to create a lean production system based on family values, excellence, continuous improvement, leadership and minimum to zero waste. The principles explained in this detailed encyclopedia, are with examples and full clarification.

This encyclopedia flows naturally and synchronously, just like the process that it is describing. You can implement these principles in any business that requires:

1. **Employee Involvement**

2. **Continuous Improvement**

3. **Standardized Processes**

4. **Reducing Waste**

5. **Leveling Workflow**

6. **Learn How to Avoid Mistakes**

One of the misnomers in regards to the success of Toyota Production System (TPS) is that it is based mainly on a "Lean Management System". The fact is that "Lean Management

System" is only one cog in the mechanism that makes up the environment and the refinement as explained in this encyclopedia.

The encyclopedia, also shows how many companies go out to adapt to Toyota's viewpoint but fail as they merely implement part of it. You won't have a strong house with only the walls, you must have a strong foundation and a strong roof as well.

Organizations flaunt "Lean Management" and "Six Sigma" as if these branded programs are some form of industrial elixir. This encyclopedia reminds us quite shrewdly that TPS runs much deeper than its famous vocabulary words.

This encyclopedia is a naturally obvious option for anyone who wishes to decode the noise and understand what is really going on at the heart of Toyota's world class efficiency.

TPS was able to significantly reduce lead time and cost, whilst constantly improving quality. This made Toyota one of the ten largest companies in the world. It is currently as profitable as all the other car companies of the world put together. In 2007, Toyota became the largest car manufacturer in the world.

Toyota is the world-class leader of lean production. In difference to batch and queue systems, lean focuses on one-piece flow. The customer is the next process and the ideal batch size is one, hence the source of defects can be found before thousands of defective parts are finished. As poignantly stated by Fujio Cho, the ex-president of Toyota Motor Corporation, Kentucky, USA:

> "If you are not shutting down the assembly plant,
> it means you have no problems.
> All manufacturing plants have problems.
> So you must be hiding your problems."

Fujio Cho

BASICS OF LEAN MANAGEMENT TRAINING

The fundamental basics of a successful and effective Lean Management Training Program are as follows:

1. **Consensus on Need for Change:** The first challenge of a training program is how to rally a company-wide consensus on the subject of initiating change. To accomplish this your lean manufacturing training program must first and foremost recognise and then communicate the need for change.

2. **Commitment:** The necessary requirement for change and the need for a company-wide commitment to a paradigm shift for achieving an effective transformation.

3. **Planning and Simulation:** Vision board simulation exercises of the "before and after" are an excellent solution to establish a PDCA (Plan - Do - Check - Assess) Cycle. Pull System simulation sets up a "one- piece flow" production line using JIT (Just in Time) and Kanban's.

4. **Training:** A primary reason for a lean transformation failure is a lack of effective training on "How To" and a companywide communication channel and consensus.

5. **Identifying Root Cause and Initiating Lean Tools:** A need to develop and implement lean tools for identifying and eliminating root causes of waste.

6. **Employee Involvement:** For change to be effective a complete employee involvement is an essential prerequisite and as the adage goes:

"What I hear I forget, What I see I remember, What I do I understand."

Confucius

HOW TO GET LEAN MANAGEMENT INTO ACTION

Teams must understand and master the following without any possibility of doubt or lack of transparency:

1. How to move from "firefighting" to proactive problem solving via a **PDCA (Plan - Do - Check - Assess) Cycle**

2. How to convert an old industrial "Push System" into a "Pull System"

3. How to increase transparency via elimination of shop floor confusion and workplace stress

4. How to introduce and apply a customer driven demand flow technology

5. How to power of single flow and sequential flow production and point-of-use logistics for materials and tools

6. How to implement and sustain a Lean Manufacturing initiative

7. How to decrease scrap, rework and work-in-process inventory via a Just in Time (JIT) System

8. How to transform manufacturing training and learning from drudgery to fun

9. How to think from "inside the box" to "outside the box" to "no box at all"

PRACTICING WHAT WE TEACH

"Better to light a candle than to curse the darkness."

Chinese Proverb

A note from the author:

A question that is often asked is, "Do all Lean Management practitioners really practice what they teach?". I can usually answer yes for my part, because I care about the best practices of Lean as it has impacted my life for the better, and I sincerely value its contribution towards the development of a pragmatic and high standards culture for the multiple world class organizations that I have had the honor to train.

If you live its teachings, your credibility as a believer in its practices means that you don't want to be: that physician who chooses to smoke, but lectures you on the dangers of smoking and encourages you to stop.

If you are going to stand up in front of people and tell them how much Lean Management can improve their business as well as personal life, then you will have to back this up with a self-disciplined, principled and well-charactered approached. Personally, Lean is a way of life for me and I assure you that if you stick with it long enough, it will improve the quality of your life both as a professional as well as life in general.

I have worked with multiple multinational companies and speak from experience about how they have moved from average to satisfactory and then on to excellence via the pragmatic and disciplined application of Lean Management Best-Practices.

First and foremost, I had to grapple with the preconceived notions about what TPS was and wasn't. Helping people with building a foundation via introduction to TPS or Lean was always hard, but people who stuck with it as a prerequisite eventually succeeded. Of course, it is not easy and as that is true for all paradigm shifts. TPS is explicitly focused on a simple premise, "there's nothing more cathartic than a cleansing of the stuff in our past that weighs us down."

We all slack off, now and then. Yes of course, none of us are perfect and even the best of us have our moments of procrastination and doubt. We're human and via our realization, we have a choice about how conscious or unconscious, we want to be about our habits and actions, hence we can make a difference in our life and the lives of others. A primary question that I always ask myself is as parents, a husband, a son, a friend, a leader, a teacher, an author, a world-citizen, and most importantly as a human being, what habits do I wish to model for others to make our collective world a better place than I have found it?

Be forewarned, Lean practices are contagious and I implore you to open your heart and mind in implementing them as an overarching vision for not only yourself, your organization but also for a better and more sustainable world…

Gabriel Iqbal
Oakville, Ontario, Canada
January, 2016

TOYOTA TIMELINE

Name in English: Toyota Motor Corporation

Name in Japanese: トヨタ自動車株式会社

Headquarters: Toyota, Aichi, Japan

1934: while still a subdivision of Toyota Industries, it created its first product, the Type A engine.

1937: founded by Kiichiro Toyoda as a offshoot from his father's company Toyota Industries to create automobiles.

1936: produces its first passenger car, the Toyota AA.

2007: became the largest car manufacturer in the world.

2012: the company reported the production of its 200-millionth vehicle.

2014: the multinational corporation consisted of 338,875 employees worldwide.

2014: the eleventh-largest company in the world by revenue.

July 2014: Toyota was the largest listed company in Japan by market capitalization.

Toyota Motor Corporation produces vehicles under 5 brands: Toyota, Hino, Lexus, Ranz, and Scion.

Toyota stakes:

51.2% in Daihatsu

1. 16.66% in Fuji Heavy Industries

2. 5.9% in Isuzu

3. 3.58% in the Yamaha Motor Company

4. 0.27% in Tesla

Toyota joint-ventures:

1. Two in China (GAC Toyota and Sichuan FAW Toyota Motor)

2. India (Toyota Kirloskar)

3. Czech Republic (TPCA)

TMC is part of the Toyota Group, one of the largest conglomerates in the world.

Toyota is the world's first car manufacturer to produce more than 10 million vehicles per year.

Toyota is currently as profitable as all the other car companies of the world put together.

THE HISTORY AND PHILOSOPHY OF THE TOYOTA PRODUCTION SYSTEM

The Toyota Production System (TPS) synergises management philosophy and practices to form an integrated socio-technical system at Toyota.

The TPS is designed to coordinate manufacturing and logistics for the automobile manufacturer, that includes interaction with suppliers and customers in a leaner Pull and synchronised process called Just in Time (JIT).

The system is a major precursor of the more generic process termed, "Lean Manufacturing".

Taiichi Ohno, Shigeo Shingo and Eiji Toyoda developed the TPS between 1948 and 1975. Formerly it was called "Just In Time Production,". It builds on the approach created by the founder of Toyota, Sakichi Toyoda, his son Kiichiro Toyoda, and the engineer Taiichi Ohno. It is said that these founders of Toyota incorporated heavily from the work of W. Edwards Deming and the writings of Henry Ford. While on a trip to the US to observe the assembly line and mass production that had made Ford rich, they were not convinced about various operational issue. They first visited various Ford plants in Michigan. Ford was the industry leader at that time. They found many of the processes in use, to be not very effective, and that there was a large amounts of inventory on site. The flow of work performed in various departments within the factory was generally not uniform. However, while shopping in at Piggly Wiggly, a supermarket, they observed the simple idea of an automatic drink resupplier; when the customer wants a drink, he/she takes one, and it is thus automatically replaced. This idea stuck with them and they went home to re-engineer the TPS using this methodology. They were quickly motivated by the idea as to how the supermarket only reordered and restocked goods once they'd been bought by customers.

Toyota applied the lesson from Piggly Wiggly Super Market, hence reducing the amount of inventory they would hold only to an amount that its employees would need for a small period of time, and then subsequently reorder based on the customer demand. This is what lead to the famous Just-in-Time (JIT) inventory system.

Low inventory levels are a basic outcome of the Toyota Production System. However, an important element of the philosophy behind its system is to continuously improve the work flow and eliminate waste 'Muda' so that production is optimised and large inventories are not necessary.

WHY SOME COMPANIES FAIL TO ADAPT THE TOYOTA PRODUCTION SYSTEM

"Knowing is not enough, we must apply.
Willing is not enough, we must do."

Bruce Lee

TPS has been compared to squeezing water from a dry towel. This means that it is a process of thorough waste elimination. Here, waste refers to anything which does not add value and does not continuously advance the process. People generally settle for eliminating the waste that everyone recognises as obvious waste. However, that is not enough, as waste is not just in terms of physical waste, it is in terms of time and process flow as well. Most people do not see that and are willing to tolerate it, as it is not obvious.

Various American businesses, having observed Toyota's success, tried to copy the system with low inventory levels, without understanding what made these reductions feasible. These projects ended in failure as the act of imitating without understanding the underlying concept or motivation was probably a recipe for disaster.

Continuous improvement (Kaizen) is a work philosophy that forms the backbone of innovation and change, however, people become accustomed to old ways of doing things without questioning the system. TPS goes back to basics, exposing the real significance of problems and then making fundamental improvements, which most companies that try to mimic Toyota fail to understand and hence lack application.

TOYOTA PARABLE

A famous parable often quoted as a comparative story between Toyota and an American car company is as below:

A Japanese company (Toyota) and an American car
company decided to have a canoe race on the Missouri River.
Both teams practiced long and hard to reach their peak performance before the race.

On the big day, the Japanese won by a mile.

The Americans, very discouraged and depressed, decided to investigate the reason for the crushing defeat. A management team made up of senior management was formed to investigate and recommend appropriate action.

Their conclusion was the Japanese had 8 people rowing and 1 person steering, while the American team had 8 people steering and 1 person rowing.

Feeling a deeper study was in order, American management hired a consulting company and paid them a large amount of money for a second opinion.

They advised, of course, that too many people were steering the boat,
while not enough people were rowing.

Not sure of how to utilize that information, but wanting to prevent another loss to the Japanese, the rowing team's management structure was totally reorganized to 4 steering supervisors, 3 area steering superintendents, and 1 assistant superintendent steering manager.

They also implemented a new performance system that would give the 1 person rowing the boat greater incentive to work harder. It was called the 'Rowing Team Quality First Program,' with meetings, dinners, and free pens for the rower.
There was discussion of getting new paddles, canoes, and other equipment, extra vacation days for practices and bonuses.

The next year the Japanese won by two miles.

Humiliated, the American management laid off the rower for poor performance, halted development of a new canoe, sold the paddles, and canceled all capital investments for new equipment. The money saved was distributed to the Senior Executives as bonuses and the next year's racing team was out-sourced to India .

Here's something else to think about:

The American company has spent the last thirty years moving all its factories out of the US, claiming they can't make money paying American wages.

Toyota has spent the last thirty years building more than a dozen plants inside the US. The last quarter's results: Toyota makes 4 billion in profits while as the American company racked up 9 billion in losses.

While this parable is about the car industry, it is repeated in many industries across the US, in particular, the manufacturing industry.

How can US survive as a country without a viable manufacturing industry?

US keeps on to moving or outsource manufacturing outside the country. It does so under the premise that it cannot compete with lower cost wages in different places around the world. However, Toyota is competing and running highly efficient plants in the US. Hence, the cost of labor is not the problem. The problem is the inflated management structures in US, which is usually having multiple hierarchies. Toyota is known to grow people and in the US that does not seem to be as promising a case as the top level executives are given higher precedence and bonuses while only a small amount trickles down the work force.

A Chinese proverb comes to mind:

"If you want 1 year of prosperity, grow grain.
If you want 10 years of prosperity, grow trees.
If you want 100 years of prosperity, grow people."

Chinese Proverb

THE ZEN OF LEAN

"Toyota is as much a state of mind as it is a car company."

USA Today

The true story of humanity is about self-realization, all else is just the kernel, the actual seed lies in the heart of the self-realized person. Zen Koan's are an attempt via spiritual and mystical traditions to reach for this self-realization. I hesitate to say the word "reach out" as the journey is mostly "inward" into one's own inner core, essentially the heart, or to put it more appropriately, "the heart's essence".

Zen Koan's consist of paradoxes to be meditated upon. These Koan's are like parables and are used to abandon the dependence on the mind and reach a sudden awareness via an intuitive enlightenment.

As I have understood it, the actual success of the TPS Lean Management System has its roots deep within the Japanese traditional Zen culture, that is based on discipline and self-reflection.

Even the word Samurai (侍), which is a "Japanese Sword" or "Japanese Warrior", actually in Japanese traditional culture means, "Service". Hence, we find a strong industrious culture of discipline, service and self-reflection embedded within the cultural ethos of Japan. The word Samurai has developed into the verb Saburahu (さぶらふ, To Serve or To Attend).

Following are a few Zen Koans that I have connected with the TPS from an intuitive metaphysical perspective:

Samurai Warrior on Horseback (Circa 1878)

"From no Flow, to Being Part of the Flow, to Become the Flow"

Explanation:

The TPS Flow process requires a mindset that is based on single flow as a Pull process. The TPS Pull process perfects a single flow process and then enacts it down to a science, with constant room for improvement via Kaizen (Continuous Improvement).

Effect on Decision Making:

Decide on a streamlined process via PDCA (Plan, Do, Check, Act) and follow it thoroughly from start to finish, while eliminating waste and error. Do not show any resistance to the flow and don't even try to be part of it, simply, become the flow.

> "I fear not the man who has
> practiced 10,000 kicks once,
> but I fear the man who has practiced
> one kick 10,000 times."
>
> Bruce Lee

"Knowing When Enough is Enough"

A student kept of trying to heat water for a medical preparation but just before her preparation was about to get ready, she ran out of firewood. She kept on running back and forth in resetting the preparation by getting more firewood from the forest, but every time she was met by the same shortage. She met a hermit in the forest who noticed her coming back and forth. The hermit asked her why are you so worked-up. She told him about her predicament and he paused for a while and said, "why don't you decrease the amount of water so that it is just enough for the preparation". The student had an immediate realization and obviously the experiment worked.

Explanation:

We tend to always over estimate and overdo things hence we often ruin and waste, time, energy, resources and the environment; not to mention the frustration that we bring upon ourselves. It is a skill to know and "use only what you need".

Effect on Decision Making:

Know when enough is enough and you will always have enough.

> "If you know when enough is enough
> you will always have enough."

Lao Tzu

"Be Like The Bamboo"

An athlete trained hard for a year and failed to get any medals in the world championships. He gave up for a few years, eventually deciding to give it another shot. He trained again for a year and he still did not succeed. He then met a monk in an uncanny encounter during a vacation in a strange land. The monk noticed a sad look on the athletes face as he read his soul. The monk invited him for tea in the tea garden. As they sipped the tea the monk stated, "Look at that Bamboo, tall and strong, isn't it, yet it shows no sign of growth for the first three years and suddenly in the fourth year the Bamboo shoots off and shows a phenomenal growth both in terms of strength and flexibility." The athlete learnt his lesson immediately, and trained persistently with discipline for three years in the fourth year he took part in the world championships again and won.

Explanation:

Anything that is worthwhile takes persistence. There are no short cuts in life. Express usefulness through simplicity. Commit yourself to continuous growth.

Effect on Decision Making:

Consistency and discipline is the key to success. Bend but don't break and be flexible yet firmly rooted.

> "Notice that the stiffest tree is most easily cracked,
> while the bamboo or willow survives by bending with the wind."

Bruce Lee

Painting Bamboo, by Xu Wei, Ming Dynasty (Created: 1540-1590)

"Empty Your Cup"

A Zen master was visited by a university professor who came to inquire about Zen. The Zen master served tea. He poured the professor's cup to the brim, and then kept on overflowing the cup.

The professor was surprised and complained, "what are you doing, no more will go into the cup." The Zen master kept on pouring and the professor got frustrated and shouted, "Alright, enough!"

The Zen master said in a calm manner, "Like the cup you are full of your own ideas. How can I show you Zen unless you first empty your mind?"

Explanation:

Before learning new thinks we must first learn to unlearn.

Effects on Decision Making:

New insights can only come through deconstructing the old ones. Hence, it's imperative in decision making that in order to resolve problems, a fresh perspective is always the solution.

> "Empty your mind, be formless, shapeless - like water.
> Now you put water into a cup, it becomes the cup,
> you put water into a bottle, it becomes the bottle,
> you put it in a teapot, it becomes the teapot.
> Now water can flow or it can crash. Be water, my friend."
>
> Bruce Lee

"Doing One Thing at a Time"

A monk said, "When I sleep, I sleep, when I work, I work, when I eat, I eat... I do only one thing at a time".

The disciples responded, "But we multi-task all the time as we have to keep up with everything".

"Well then", said the monk, "What is the quality of your doing?"

The disciples responded, "It's just a task and as long as we get it done, the quality does not matter".

"That is the difference between you and me", said the monk. "I meditate on everything I do, and in doing so, I do only one thing at a time, and I focus on quality, and that matters more in the long run than quantity".

The disciples realized what the monk was talking about and started working on focusing on one task in a given moment.

Explanation:

Focusing on one task improves overall long term efficiency. The true Alchemist seers refined their inner-self to Gold not the material Gold. They did this by sharpening their quality of focusing on self-actualization.

Effect on Decision Making:

Quality should never be left at the mercy of quantity.

"A person who chases two rabbits, catches none."

Confucius

"The Parable of the Tortoise and Hare"

This is a commonly well-known parable in all cultures. The tortoise and hare had a race. The tortoise took his time and moved slowly but steadily. The hare dashed forward and got exhausted and felt over-confident because of the apparent advantage he had gained and went to sleep. The tortoise in the meantime reached the final line while the hare lay deep in sleep.

Explanation:

Slow and steady wins the race. Faster is not always better.

> "There is more to life
> than increasing its speed."
>
> Gandhi

Effect on Decision Making:

We have seen this effect in many companies lately. Discipline, Planning and Strategy always pay back in the long run.

> "Nature does not hurry,
> yet everything is accomplished."
>
> Lao Tzu

WHAT IS THE TOYOTA PRODUCTION SYSTEM

"If you look up, there are no limits."

Japanese Proverb

TPS - Toyota Production System is also referred to as the Thinking People System.

PDCA

It is a system that uses the PDCA approach to involve everyone in solving problems and improving quality, cost, delivery, safety, and morale:

- P - Plan
- D - Do
- C - Check
- A - Act

The inner core of the TPS

The inner core of the TPS is explained via a "house structure" (see diagrams on next two pages). It was named so because it represented stability and structure.

TPS has been used as an Operational Blueprint for Lean Management by various successful organizations.

TOYOTA PRODUCTION SYSTEM HOUSE

Copyright © 2016 Gabriel Iqbal

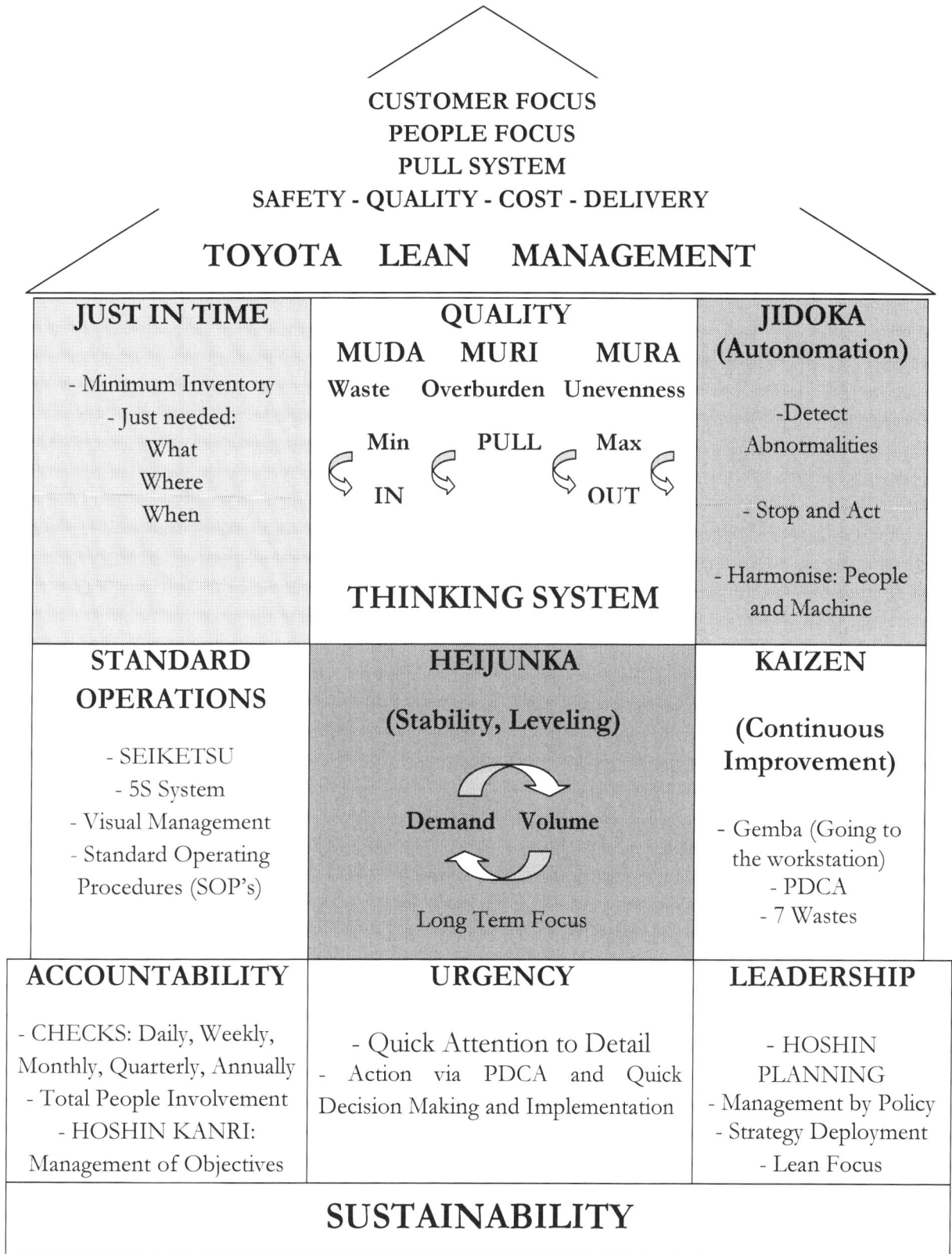

CUSTOMER FOCUS
PEOPLE FOCUS
PULL SYSTEM
SAFETY - QUALITY - COST - DELIVERY

TOYOTA   LEAN   MANAGEMENT

JUST IN TIME	QUALITY	JIDOKA (Autonomation)
- Minimum Inventory - Just needed: What Where When	MUDA MURI MURA Waste Overburden Unevenness Min PULL Max IN OUT **THINKING SYSTEM**	-Detect Abnormalities - Stop and Act - Harmonise: People and Machine
STANDARD OPERATIONS - SEIKETSU - 5S System - Visual Management - Standard Operating Procedures (SOP's)	HEIJUNKA (Stability, Leveling) Demand Volume Long Term Focus	KAIZEN (Continuous Improvement) - Gemba (Going to the workstation) - PDCA - 7 Wastes
ACCOUNTABILITY - CHECKS: Daily, Weekly, Monthly, Quarterly, Annually - Total People Involvement - HOSHIN KANRI: Management of Objectives	URGENCY - Quick Attention to Detail - Action via PDCA and Quick Decision Making and Implementation	LEADERSHIP - HOSHIN PLANNING - Management by Policy - Strategy Deployment - Lean Focus

SUSTAINABILITY

Note: The author has adapted the above model from the original TPS House

TOYOTA PRODUCTION SYSTEM PILLARS

Left Pillar	**Just-in-Time (Takt Time-Flow-Pull)** (ジャストインタイム) Takt time is the pace at which the client is buying a special merchandise or service. Takt time is the total net daily available "operating" time divided by the total daily customer demand. Eliminates the 7 Wastes of Production. Designs a smooth flow of product and information, minimizes inventory and space.
Right Pillar	**Jidoka (Autonomation)** (自働化) Builds quality into the process, separates human and machine processes using intelligent automation. Implements low-cost automation, error-proofing, equipment upgrades and reliability improvement.
Foundation	**Heijunka (Leveling)** (平準化) Stabilizes production schedule variability Reduces total Lead-time, coordinates sales, scheduling, and customer needs and demands.

Note: The author has adapted the above model from the original TPS Pillars

BASIC 15 PRINCIPLES

"By denying scientific principles,
one may maintain any paradox."

Galileo Galilei

Upon reflection on Toyota's best practices, the basic 15 principles that you could use as the keystone for your organisation are:

1. **SUSTAINABLE DEVELOPMENT**: Short-term goals should never be held hostage at the helm of long term goals. Therefore set your objectives on a long-term philosophy even at the expense of less financial gains. This sets a culture of sustainable development as a high priority.

2. **STANDARDIZATION (SEIKETSU):** Standardized tasks are the groundwork for continuous improvement, therefore set up visuals for standardized processes. To bring problems to the surface set up a *Continuous Process Flow*.

3. **PULL SYSTEM:** Use Pull System to avoid overproduction.

4. **LEVEL OUT THE WORKLOAD (HIEJUNKA):** Work like the tortoise and not the hare, hence, level out the workload precisely, uniformly and evenly.

5. **5S SYSTEM:** It is the definitive guide to an organised workplace. 5S's are the five keys to Total Quality Environment. These are: Sorting Out (Seiri), Arrangement (Seiton), Cleanliness (Seiso), Standardization (Seiketsu), and Sustaining Discipline (Shitsuke).

6. **DECISION MAKING:** Build collective decisions by consensus building, and then by fully considering all options and further implement the decisions rapidly via the people involved.

7. **VISUAL CARDS (KANBAN) / TRAFFIC LIGHTS (ANDON):** Use visual control so no problems are obscured. Toyota is focused fundamentally on process as well as technology. "***Often the best option was a low-tech solution.***" Visual Cards (Kanban) are used to signal replenishment of parts. Traffic lights (Andon) are used to signal production line problems and shut downs. For Toyota, "***Technology should be highly visual and intuitive.***"

8. **STOP WHEN THERE IS A PROBLEM (JIDOKA) / MISTAKE PROOFING (POKA YOKE):** To get quality right the first time, set-up a culture of stopping to fix problems even at the cost of bring a stop to the entire process. Counter-intuitively, Toyota does not attempt for zero downtime. The production line is deliberately stopped when there is a problem (Jidoka), so that problems are highlighted and corrected without a chain reaction of errors building up further. Hence Mistake Proofing (Poka Yoke), has a very high priority.

9. **LEADERSHIP DEVELOPMENT:** Grow leaders who meticulously realize the work, live the beliefs, and facilitate it to others.

10. **TESTED TECHNOLOGY / SIMPLIFIED AND HIGHLY ANIMATED FORMAT:** Use only reliable, visual, thoroughly tested technology that serves your people and processes in a simplified and highly animated format.

11. **TRANSPARENCY**: Be transparent and respect your extended network of partners, suppliers and customers.

12. **THREE MAIN STRENGTHS OF TPS:** The main principles of TPS are **CONTINUOUS IMPROVEMENT (KAIZEN)** and **REDUCING WASTE (MUDA)** such as unnecessary work, uneven workflow, and excess inventory. While **JUST-IN-TIME (JIT)** inventory enables efficient production, but not without vulnerabilities. Toyota maintains a very deep relationship with its suppliers as well as customers and is very transparent about its Corrective Action, Process Improvement and hence a pioneer in setting up full transparency for recall or defect correction.

13. **GENCHI GENBUTSU (GOING TO THE ROOT OF THE PROBLEM):** An idea which resonates is Genchi Genbutsu. You cannot be certain you actually realize any piece of any problem unless you go out of your way to find out for yourself firsthand the source of the problem. Carefully understand the situation by going and seeing for yourself (Genchi Genbutsu) at the source of the problem.

14. **CONSENSUS BUILDING (NEMAWASHI)** It is an integral part of Toyota's disciplined and people focused culture. In essence, everyone affected by a decision must be consulted in full view of the "problem-solution paradigm" in advance. This minimizes unanticipated obstacles impeding execution of processes and the staff remain fully on board and proactively offer Continuous Improvement (Kaizen) solutions. A Chinese proverb explains this: "Tell me and I'll forget; show me and I may remember; involve me and I'll understand."

15. **RELENTLESS REFLECTION (HANSEI):** Create a culture of Relentless Reflection and continuous improvement (Kaizen). Consistently adding value to the organization by developing processes, people and partners.

A quote from Fujio Cho, puts it all together:

"Since Toyota's founding we have adhered to the core principle of contributing to society through the practice of manufacturing high-quality products and services. Our business practices and activities based on this core principle created values, beliefs and business methods that over the years have become a source of competitive advantage. These are managerial values and business methods that are known collectively as the Toyota Way"

Fujio Cho, President Toyota (2001)

PROCESS OBJECTIVES

"We are what we repeatedly do.
Excellence, then, is not an act, but a habit."

Aristotle

The primary objectives of the TPS are:

(1) Just in Time or Lean Manufacturing

(2) Total Quality

(3) Total Preventative Maintenance

1) **Just in Time or Lean Manufacturing**

The step by step detection and deletion of waste. Waste in this meaning is defined as, any activity that adds cost, but not value to the end product, such as:

a) **Excess production**

b) **Stock**

c) **Idle work in progress**

d) **Unnecessary movement**

e) **Scrap**

2) **Total Quality**

Setting up a proactive culture of intolerance to defects both in the procedures and also information such as bills of material and inventory books. Total quality is often referred to as Six Sigma which uses total quality and lean manufacturing techniques to attempt to reduce rejects to 3.4 per million parts produced.

3) **Total Preventative Maintenance**

Following a Standard Operating Procedure (SOP) for preventative maintenance to ensure quality, safety and environmental protection. A preventative maintenance program means that unplanned stoppages due to equipment failure are minimised.

OVERBURDEN, INCONSISTENCY, AND ELIMINATING WASTE

"Your beliefs become your thoughts,
Your thoughts become your words,
Your words become your actions,
Your actions become your habits,
Your habits become your values,
Your values become your destiny."

Gandhi

The main goals of the TPS are to rule out the following in their design process:

(1) Overburden (Muri)

(2) Inconsistency (Mura)

(3) Eliminate Waste (Muda)

- Muda (Japanese: 無駄 or ムダ) (English: Waste)

- Mura (Japanese: 斑 or ムラ) (English: Unevenness)

- Muri (Japanese: 無理) (English: Overburden)

The largest effects on process value delivery are achieved by designing a process that is able to bring the required results effortlessly; by designing out:

- **Inconsistency** "Mura".

- Next in line is to make certain that the process can flex as much as required without stress or **Overburden** "Muri" since this generates **Waste** "Muda".

- Finally the tactical continuous improvements of waste reduction or the **Elimination of Waste** "Muda" are very valuable.

TPS focuses on 7 kinds of wastes, "Muda":

1. **Over-production**

2. **Motion (operator or machine)**

3. **Waiting (operator or machine)**

4. **Conveyance**

5. **Processing itself**

6. **Inventory (raw material)**

7. **Correction (rework and scrap)**

5S SYSTEM

"Sow a thought, reap an action; sow an action, reap a habit;
sow a habit, reap a character; sow a character, reap a destiny."

Stephen R. Covey, The 7 Habits of Highly Effective People

It is a methodology for organizing a workplace, especially a collective workplace (a shop floor or an office space etc), and maintaining its organized state. 5S is far more sophisticated than housekeeping. It's erroneously referred to as a housekeeping process, as this description is deceptive.

5S is a citation to a list of five Japanese terms which when translated and transliterated into English, start with the letter S.

5S as a mnemonic seeks to translate information into a form that the brain can retain better than its original form. The 5S list is a mnemonic for a process that is often erroneously categorized as "standardized cleanup", as its much more than that. It is a complete disciplined philosophy and a path of organising and managing the "workspace" and "work flow" with the intent to "improve efficiency" by "eliminating waste", "improving streamlining" and "decreasing process awkwardness".

5S Flow Chart

5 PILLARS OF VISUAL WORKPLACE

5S's are the five keys to Total Quality Environment

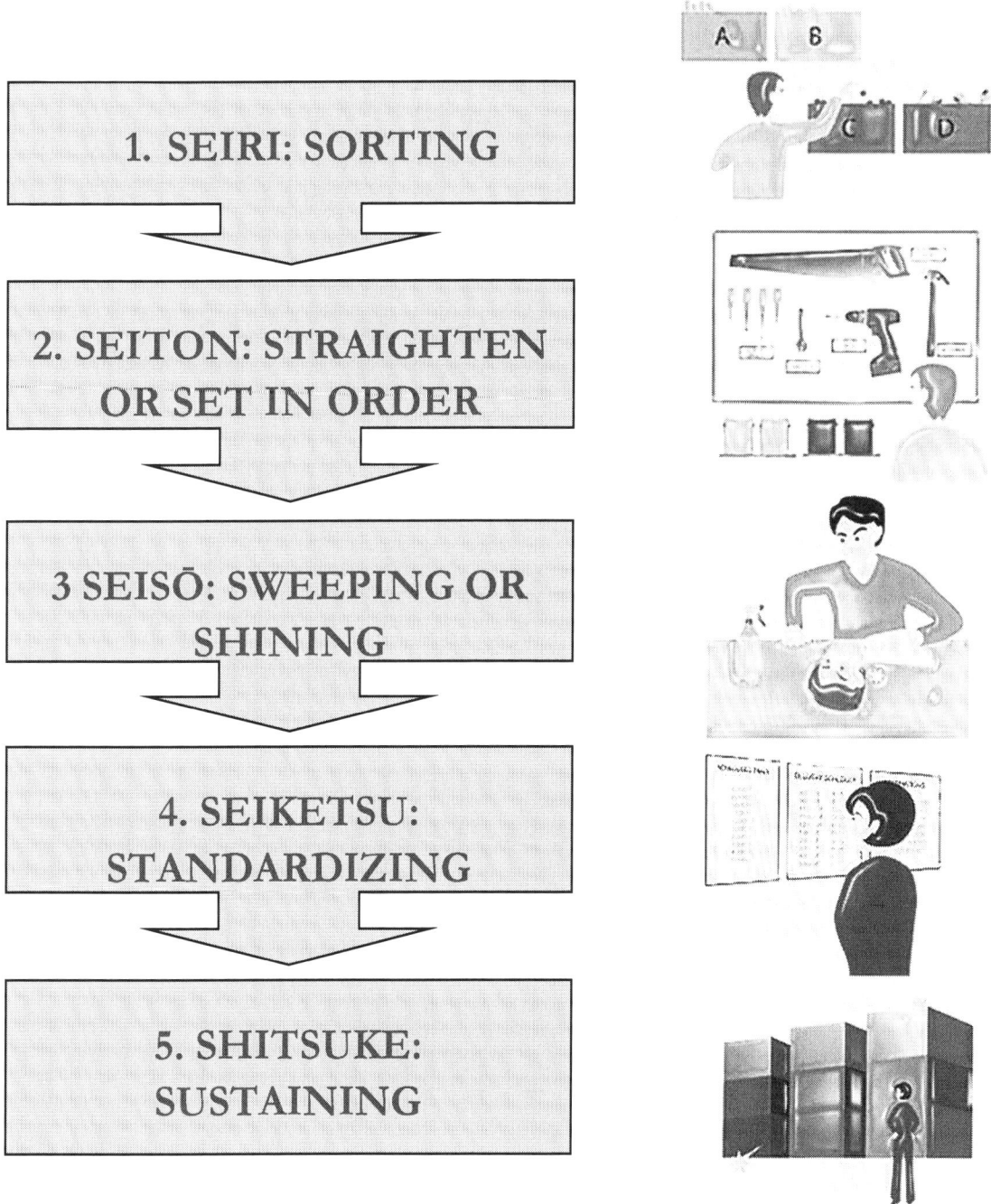

1. SEIRI: SORTING

2. SEITON: STRAIGHTEN OR SET IN ORDER

3 SEISŌ: SWEEPING OR SHINING

4. SEIKETSU: STANDARDIZING

5. SHITSUKE: SUSTAINING

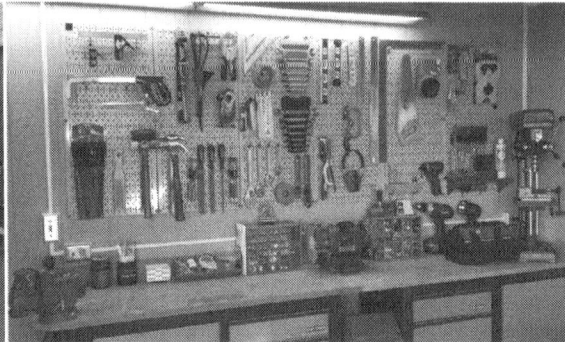

Before

After

5S at Work

Assembling with white gloves.

Easy access to tools

Visual alarm that indicates problems.

THE AIMS OF 5S

1. An essential step required for Waste Elimination

2. An integral step in Kaizen

3. Improve workplace morale and efficiency

4. Assigning everything a set location, hence time is not wasted by looking for things. Further it is promptly noticeable when something is missing from its set place

5. The payback of this method come from collectively settling on:

   a) **What** should be kept

   b) **Where** it should be kept

   c) **How** it should be stored

6. The collectively settling on process usually comes from a discussion about standardization. Hence, setting up a clear understanding, among people, on how to organize the work place.

7. Builds ownership of the process in each person.

8. Set up an order for items and activities in such a manner so that we can promote a leaner work flow:

a) **Accessible:** Tools should be kept at the set place after use and should be easily accessible.

b) **Ergonomics:** Ergonomical and minimum effort should be used to access the tools.

c) **Work Flow:** Flow paths can be always changed to improve efficiency and effectiveness via Kaizen.

DESCRIBING 5S

STAGE 1 - SEIRI (整理) SORTING:

American

SORT Evaluate and eliminate everything not required for the current work, keeping only the bare essentials that are needed.

Japanese

Seiri 'Say-ree' (Organization) Separate needed tools, parts, and instructions from unneeded materials and instantly remove the latter unnecessary things and send them off for recycling, storage or waste.

Checking all the tools, materials, accessories etc, in the shop-floor and work area and **maintaining only the items that are Essential.** Everything else is either discarded, recycled and only if need be, stored.

Meaning: Putting things in order, Sorting, Removing what is not needed and keeping what is needed.

Activities:

1. Sort through and then sort out

2. Identify which items are required

3. Discard what is unnecessary

Guidelines:

1. Things we don't use: discard.

2. Things we don't use but want to have on hand just-in-case: Keep as contingency items.

3. Things we use only infrequently: store somewhere far away

4. Things we use sometimes: store in workplace

5. Things we use frequently: keep at workplace or on the person

STAGE 2 - SEITON (整頓) STRAIGHTEN OR SET IN ORDER:

American

SET IN ORDER (Straighten)   Arrange items in a way that they are easily visible, accessible with lest amount of time required to find them and ergonomically feasible.

Japanese

Seiton 'Say-ton' (Tidiness)   Put things in order: Neatly arrange and identify materials and equipment/tools for ease of use in a practical and flexible manner.

This stage focuses on efficiency and flow. **Arrange** the tools, materials, equipment and parts in a manner that promotes the best possible flow of work. Everything should be kept and maintained at designated places and where they will be used hence straightening the flow path. Therefore the process is optimized to set in an **organized flow and order that maximizes efficiency and effectiveness**.

Meaning: Keep things in such a manner that people can reach them easily whenever they need.

Activities:

1. Design/plan Functional Storage based upon 5W1H (What-Where-When-Who-How-Why) Method for Cause-effect Analysis.

2. Create place for everything and everything in its place

3. Keep accessibility as easy as possible, also minimum material handling

4. Zoning and placement marks

5. First In First Out (FIFO)

PROBLEMS TO BE AVOIDED

1. MOTION WASTE

2. SEARCHING WASTE

3. THE WASTE OF HUMAN ENERGY

4. THE WASTE OF EXCESS INVENTORY

5. THE WASTE OF UNSAFE CONDITIONS

IMPLEMENTATION

DECIDING APPROPRIATE LOCATIONS

- PRINCIPLES OF STORING JIGS, TOOLS AND DIES
- PRINCIPLES OF MOTION ECONOMY
- VISUAL CONTROLS

PRINCIPLES OF STORING JIGS, TOOLS AND DIES

1. FREQUENCY OF USE

2. SEQUENCE OF USE

3. EASE OF HANDLING

4. VARIETY ELIMINATION OF JIGS AND DIES

5. STORE TOOLS BY PRODUCT

PRINCIPLES OF MOTION ECONOMY

1. AVOID ZIGZAG AND CHANGE IN DIRECTION

2. USE FOOT OPERATED SWITCHES

3. KEEP MATERIAL AND TOOLS IN FRONT AND IN ORDER OF USE

4. OPERATOR AT PROPER HEIGHT

5. POSITION PARTS AND MATERIAL FOR EASY REACH

6. PROPER HANDLES AND GRIPS

VISUAL CONTROLS

A visual control is any communication device used in the work environment that tells us at a glance how work should be done

1. SIGN BOARD STRATEGY

2. PAINTING STRATEGY

3. COLOUR CODING STRATEGY

4. OUTLINING STRATEGY

STAGE 3 - SEISŌ (清掃) SWEEPING OR SHINING:

American

SHINE (Sweep) Inspect, refine, and clean everything and find ways to maintain it and keep it clean. Make this a part of your everyday best practice.

Japanese

Seiso 'Say-soo' (Purity) Conduct a cleanup campaign. Clean to original condition promptly and frequently. Do cleaning work positively with a good and positive attitude.

Top priority is given to **Systematic Cleaning**. At the end of each shift, and even during the operation each specific work area is cleaned up by the respective staff and **everything is restored to its original designated area.** This is very important as it brings clarity and promotes a culture of "**clean as you go**".

Meaning: Keeping things clean and polished, no dirt anywhere in the workplace.

Guidelines:

1. Why cleaning is important

2. Turn work places into clean, bright place – enjoy working

3. Keep everything in top condition so that when someone needs to use something it is ready to be used

4. Cleaning should become a daily habit like bathing

ACTIVITIES

1. Clean equipment, tools, furniture, notice boards, records etc.

2. Keep the workplace spotlessly clean.

3. Locating (inspection) and attending to minor

4. problems while cleaning.

5. Sweeping, wiping, polishing, painting etc.

6. Everybody acting like a caretaker.

7. Clean even places most people do not notice

THE THREE-WAY APPROACH

MACRO

Cleaning everything and dealing with the overall causes

INDIVIDUAL

Cleaning specific work places and specific piece of machinery

MICRO

Cleaning specific parts and tools and the causes of grime are identified and corrected

IMPLEMENTING CLEANLINESS

1. DETERMINE CLEANLINESS TARGETS

2. WAREHOUSE ITEMS

3. EQUIPMENT

4. SPACE

5. DETERMINE CLEANLINESS ASSIGNMENTS

6. 5S ASSIGNMENT MAP

7. 5S SCHEDULE

8. DETERMINE CLEANLINESS METHODS

9. DECIDE CLEANLINESS TARGETS AND TOOLS

10. STANDARDS FOR CLEANLINESS PROCEDURES

11. IMPLEMENT CLEANLINESS

TYPES OF EQUIPMENT PROBLEM

1. OIL LEAKS

2. DIRTY - OPERATOR RELUCTANT

3. GAUGES AND INDICATORS NOT ACCESSIBLE AND NOT EASY TO READ

4. NUTS AND BOLTS MISSING OR LOOSE

5. MOTORS OVERHEAT

6. SPARKS FLARE FROM POWER CORDS

7. V BELTS LOOSE OR BROKEN

8. STRANGE NOISE

STEPS IN CLEANLINESS INSPECTION

1. DETERMINE CLEANLINESS TARGETS

2. MACHINES AND EQUIPMENTS

3. JIGS, TOOLS AND DIES, GAUGES

4. ASSIGN CLEANLINESS INSPECTION JOBS

5. MAINLY WORKERS, SUPERVISORS AND GROUP LEADERS

6. LARGE SIGNBOARD FOR SHOP AND SMALL FOR EACH MACHINE

7. DECIDE CLEANLINESS INSPECTION CHECKLISTS

8. IMPLEMENT CLEANLINESS INSPECTION

STAGE 4 - SEIKETSU (清潔) STANDARDIZING:

American

STANDARDIZE (Systematize)   Create rules and SOP's by which the first 3 S's are maintained. Document the SOP's with continuous updates.

Japanese

Seiketsu 'Say-kit-sue' (Cleanliness) Conduct the other 3Ss at frequently as possible on a daily basis, in order to maintain a work environment in perfect condition, free from bad habits and procrastination.

Setting up of a **Standardized Operating Procedures (SOP's),** a manual that incorporates the process as well as quality and environmental and safety standards. This is followed via **visuals** which break down the work process **demonstrably**. If a new staff member is introduced to the process, they should be able to follow the process simply by following the SOP's. This then forms the backbone of a sophisticated work culture.

STAGE 5 - SHITSUKE (躾) SUSTAINING / SELF-DISCIPLINE:

American

SUSTAINING (Self-discipline) Keep the other 4S activities from disentanglement.

Japanese

Shitsuke 'Shit-zuk-ay'(Discipline)   Be disciplined. Form the habit of always practicing the first four Ss. Maintain what has been accomplished. Be well-mannered and use polite behavioral skills.

Maintaining and reviewing standards. Maintain the focus on the above 4'S and looking out for any slacking away of the established process. Upgrading the process via a new way of working, a new tool or a new output requirement, can be systematically introduced via a Kaizen hence reviewing any of the SOP's.

Meaning: Inspiring pride in the workplace and thorough adherence to standards in the other four components. Maintaining cleanliness, after cleaning eliminating germs and stains; also standardization.

Activities:

1. Create good awareness about 5S – Training to everyone

2. Develop norms: e.g.., one minute 5S, Exercise time, Group cleaning

3. Preparation of 5S manuals

4. Communication and feedback

5. Individual responsibility and total employee involvement

6. Practicing good habits

7. Regular monitoring through audits

8. Establish management standards for maintaining the 5Ss

9. Introduce innovative visible management

10. Color coded pipes, warning colors, inspection marks

11. Early detection and early action

12. Okay marks, Marking on meters

13. Belt size labels

14. Fire extinguisher signs

CONTINUOUS EFFECTIVE STANDARDISED CLEANUP

1. **BY TAKING TO NEXT LEVEL OF PREVENTION USING 5W1H APPROACH** (What-Where-When-Who-How-Why) Method for Cause-effect Analysis.

2. **PREVENTIVE ORGANISATION**

3. **PREVENTIVE ORDERLINESS**

4. **PREVENTIVE CLEANLINESS**

IMPLEMENTING DISCIPLINE

1. AWARENESS OF 5 PILLARS AND DISCIPLINE TO IMPLEMENTATION

2. ALLOCATE ENOUGH TIME IN WORK SCHEDULE FOR 5 PILLAR IMPLEMENTATION

3. STRUCTURE TO IMPLEMENT 5 PILLARS

4. SUPPORT FROM MANAGEMENT BY WAY OF ACKNOWLEDGEMENT, LEADERSHIP AND RESOURCES

5. REWARDS AND RECOGNITIONS

TOOLS AND TECHNIQUES FOR PROMOTING DISCIPLINE

1. 5S SLOGANS

2. 5S POSTERS

3. 5S PHOTO EXHIBITION

4. 5S NEWSLETTERS

5. 5S POCKET MANUALS

6. 5S MONTHS

MANAGEMENT ROLE

1. EDUCATING EVERYONE ON 5S CONCEPTS, TOOLS AND TECHNIQUE

2. CREATING TEAMS FOR 5S IMPLEMENTATION

3. ALLOWING TIME FOR IMPLEMENTATION AND CREAT SCHEDULES

4. PROVIDE RESOURCES

5. ACKNOWLEDGE AND SUPPORT 5S EFFORTS

6. ENCOURAGE   CREATIVE   INVOLVEMENT   BY   ALLWORKERS, LISTENING TO THEM AND ACTING ON THEM

7. PROMOTING TANGIBLE AND INTANGIBLE REWARDS

8. CONTINUOUS PROMOTION OF 5S EFFORTS (ONGOING)

9. 5S PREPARATION

10. 5S IMPLEMENTATION PREPARATION

VISION STATEMENT AND DISPLAY

1. SIGNATURE COMPAIGN

2. TARGET DATE

3. SELECT TEAM LEADERS AND MEMBERS

4. PREPARE ORGANISATION STRUCTURE

5. 5S MAP (ZONE MAP) AND DISPLAY

6. PREPARE 5S MANUAL

7. 5S AWARENESS PROGRAM

8. IDENTIFY 5S CORNER

IMPLEMENTATION

1. Only after good introduction to all members, start on a special day with all employees

2. Fix the target date for each zone

3. Review the progress periodically from the audit report

4. Take corrective action for the problems

A sixth Stage namely, **"Safety" has been** added. It is however arguable as adding it is not necessary given that following 5S accurately will produce an environment and culture that is safe.

Training and Development

Continuous education is required in order to ensure that everybody complies with the latest SOP's There and hence maintain the standards.

Changes

Changes that will affect the 5S programme -- such as new equipment, new products or new work rules etc, it is essential to make changes in the SOP's and subsequently provide training.

Visuals

A naturally effective way to continue educating employees and maintaining standards is to use 5S posters and signs along with SOP visuals

WHY 5S ?

1. **Helps in TPM Implementation**

2. **Reducing M/C Downtime**

3. **Safety**

4. **Establishes an Ambience for Quality**

5. **Creates a Healthier Corporate Climate**

6. **Better Operational Control of Process**

7. **It is a Scientific Method for Good Housekeeping**

HOUSEKEEPING

Housekeeping is a process wherein everyone in the company is committed to and involved in up keeping of the workplace and cleanliness of m/c, material etc., such that only needed material is kept and it's fastest accessibility is ensured

5 LEVELS OF HOUSEKEEPING

Level 1:
- Floor is full of unwanted material

Level 2:
- Clutter found on the walls

Level 3:
- Factory / office is clean but tools, papers, files and material disorganized

Level 4:
- Storage area, m/c, offices are clean and furniture, documents and material organized

Level 5:
- Factory / office is immaculate

RESISTANCE TO IMPLEMENT THE 5 S

1. What is so great about orderliness.

2. Why clean when it just gets dirty.

3. Implementation will not boost output.

4. We have already implemented.

5. We did the 5 S years ago.

6. We are too busy to spend time.

7. Why do we need to implement?

BENEFITS OF IMPLEMENTING 5 PILLARS

- INDIVIDUAL AND ORGANISATION
- BENEFITS TO INDIVIDUAL

INDIVIDUAL AND ORGANISATION

1. Make your workplace more Pleasant to work in

2. Make your job more satisfying

3. Remove many obstacles and frustration in your work

4. Help you to know your work and also when and where to do it

5. Makes it easier to communicate with everyone

BENEFITS TO ORGANISATION

1. Zero defects bring higher Quality

2. Zero waste brings lower Cost

3. Zero delay bring reliable Deliveries

4. Zero injury Promote Safety

5. Zero breakdowns bring better equipment availability

6. Zero complaints bring greater Confidence and Trust

SEVEN WASTES

1. **WASTE FROM OVER PRODUCTION**

2. **WAITING TIME**

3. **TRANSPORTATION**

4. **PROCESS**

5. **INVENTORY**

6. **UNWANTED MOTION**

7. **PRODUCTION DEFECTS**

NEAT AND CLEAN FACTORY HAS:

1. HIGHER PRODUCTIVITY

2. LESSER DEFECTS

3. BETTER DELIVERIES

4. IMPROVED SAFETY

5. HIGH MORALE

6. LOWER COST

PROBLEMS FACED

When Workplace is not organized properly the following problems arise:

1. Shop-floor more crowded and hard to work in

2. Storage cupboards and lockers used for storage of unwanted items will affect communication between employees

3. Time lost while searching for parts, tools etc

4. Excess inventory of parts, tools and machine result in increased cost

5. Unwanted items in shop-floor make it harder to improve the process flow

IMPLEMENTING FIRST 'S' RED TAG STRATEGY

1. **Red Tag is put on all potentially unneeded items**

2. **Evaluate and decide**

An item with red tag - Ask three questions:

1. **Is this item needed?**

2. **If it is needed, is it needed in this quantity?**

3. **If it is needed, does it need to be located here?**

After Evaluation the item may be:

1. Held in Red Tag Holding Area for a period of time to decide whether they are:

   a) **Needed**

   b) **Not Needed**

   c) **Disposed**

   d) **Relocated**

STEPS IN RED TAGGING:

1. Launch Red Tag Project

2. Identify Red Tag targets

3. Set Red Tag criteria

4. Make Red Tags

5. Attach Red Tags

6. Evaluate Red Tagged items

7. Document the results of Red Tagging

RED TAG TARGETS

1. Physical areas

2. Inventory

3. Equipment

1. PHYSICAL AREAS

- Production area
- Walls, shelves
- Warehouses
- Walkways

2. INVENTORY

- Raw material
- In Process
- Sub Assembly
- Semi Finished
- Finished

3. EQUIPMENT

- Machines
- Equipments
- Jigs and Tools
- Cutting Tools
- Gauges
- Worktable
- Cabinets, desks, chairs

RED-TAG CRITERIA

1. The usefulness of the item to perform the work

2. The frequency – it is needed

3. The quantity of the item needed to perform the work

MAKE THE RED TAGS

1. **RED TAG INFORMATIONS**

2. **CATEGORY**

3. **ITEM NAME**

4. **QUANTITY**

5. **REASONS**

6. **VALUE**

7. **DATE**

EVALUATE THE RED-TAG ITEMS

1. Keep the item where it is

2. Move the item to a new location in the work area

3. Store the item away from the work area

4. Hold the item in the red tag holding area for evaluation

5. Dispose the item

DISPOSAL METHODS

1. Throw away - as scrap or incinerate

2. Sell

3. Return to source

4. Lend to other departments-Temporary basis

5. Distribute to other Units-permanent

6. Central Red Tag area for decision

TYPES OF UNWANTED ITEMS

1. Defective or excess parts

2. Obsolete or broken Jig, tools and gauges

3. Worn out tools

4. Unsafe or broken electrical units

5. Outdated poster, signs, notices and memos

PLACES WHERE UNWANTED ITEMS ACCUMULATE

1. No man's Land

2. Corners near entrance and exit

3. Along interior and exterior walls, next to partitions and behind pillars

4. Under desk, shelves and cabinets

5. Unused exhibit boards

UNDERSTANDING AND APPLYING LEAN MANAGEMENT - AN ENCYCLOPEDIC APPROACH

"If you wish to learn the highest truths, begin with the alphabet."

Japanese Proverb

A

A THREE REPORT

A "A3" sized (11 inches x 17 inches) form is used at Toyota as a single-sheet for:

1. **Problem Evaluation**

2. **Root Cause Analysis**

3. **Corrective Action Planning**

It often includes sketches, graphics, flow maps or other visual means of summarizing the current condition and future state of the process. It is evidence of a Solution Oriented thinking for continuous improvement and problem solving.

A THREE THINKING

A3 Thinking is not the same as A3 Report. The A3 report is the evidence of A3 logical thinking based on the empirical scientific methodology and problem-solving, on a PDCA (Plan-Do-Check-Act) cycle. Its power derives from the continuous development and nurturing of a dynamic PDCA culture. The strength of the A3 report is its reflection of the process leading to its refinement, evolution and management.

A3 Thinking facilitates:

1. **Objective Thinking**

2. **Consistent and systematic thinking**

3. **Integrates and visualizes (visual communication) via a concise, understandable learning framework**

4. **Beckon for alignment, buy-in, and systems thinking through a proactive solution oriented dialogue**

A3 Thinking becomes dynamic only when it is absorbed as an integral part of the management philosophy and operations.

ABNORMALITY MANAGEMENT

A proactive work culture in which one is able to pick up and quickly take action to correct abnormalities (any straying from Standard Work).

This is the primary goal of standardization and visual management.

Continuous waste elimination and a proactive problem solving approach via Kaizen are only possible when the abnormalities are made visible and hence corrective action is taken.

ACTIVITY-BASED COSTING (ABC)

A management accounting system that allocates cost to products based on the resources used to perform a process. For example:

1. **Design**

2. **Order Entry**

3. **Production**

These resources include:

1. **Floor Space**

2. **Raw Materials**

3. **Energy**

4. **Machine Time**

5. **Labor**

ANDON

Japanese: 行灯

English: Signboard

Andon is one of the primary tools of Jidoka (Autonomation / See Section on Jidoka). An instrument of visual management, originating from the Japanese word for 'Lamp'.

A visual control system that exposes the current state of work. For example:

1. **Abnormal Conditions**

2. **Work Instructions**

3. **Job Progress Information**

In the manufacturing world, sometimes a cord that a worker can pull to stop the assembly line when they detect a defect, hence it is a line/process stop.

Most commonly, Andons are lights placed on machines or on production lines to indicate the status of the operation.

Andons are often color-coded:

1. **Green - Normal Operations**

2. **Yellow - Changeover or planned maintenance**

3. **Red – Abnormal / Machine Malfunction**

They are often mixed with an audible signal such as music or alarms.

ANDON BOARD

It is a visual control device in a work area, such as shop floor, usually with a lighted overhead display, that shows the current status of the process / system and warns team members with any emerging problems in the manufacturing process.

AUTONOMATION

Autonomation is one of the pillars of the TPS.

A process that allows stopping of a line, automatically, when a defective part is detected. Machines are programmed and are able to detect and prevent defects via an automatic process. Machines stop automatically, when defects are made, and an alarm for help is indicated. Autonomation was pioneered by Sakichi Toyoda, via the invention of automatic looms that stopped when a thread broke, hence allowing an operator to manage many looms simultaneously without the risk of producing large amounts of defective cloth. Hence corrective action is remedied promptly via an automatic set-up.

See JIDOKA, ANDON

AUTOMATIC TIME

The time when a machine/equipment is running on auto cycle and a person does not need to be there to operate the machine.

Commonly used for NC (Numerical Code) machine cycles, such as:

1. **Printers**

2. **Castings and Moulds**

3. **Oven cycles**

4. **Wash cycles**

5. **Copiers**

B

BACK FLUSHING

The goal of back flushing is to reduce the number of non value-added transactions.

A system of recording accounting transactions for labor and materials based on what was shipped as opposed to using material issues or cards.

BALANCED PLANT

An office/program/production/inventory where the capacity of all resources are balanced exactly with customer demand.

BALANCED SCORECARD

In the early 1990's the Balanced Scorecard was created by Dr. Robert Kaplan and Dr. David Norton.

The Balance Scorecard provides a macro and micro view of an organizations overall performance.

The Balanced Scorecard is a strategic management system used to drive the following throughout the organization:

1. Performance

2. Accountability

It is an organizational strategy by virtue of which an organizational framework for implementing and managing strategy at all levels of an enterprise are linked to objectives and initiatives, that are measured against an organization's strategy.

The Balance Scorecard balances operational performance and/or financial indices with more forward-looking indicators in four key dimensions:

1. Financial

2. Integration/Operational Excellence

3. Employees

4. Customers

It integrates financial measures with other key performance indicators such as:

1. Customer Perspectives

2. Internal Business Processes

3. Organizational Growth

4. Learning and Development

5. Innovation

BATCH

Making products or doing activities in groups, lots, or batches in which each part or finished good in the batch is identical. Can happen in both office/administration and production environments. The TPS does not operate via this process as it creates 'waste'. The TPS uses the Continuous Flow / Pull Method instead that is based on customer demand as opposed to creation of products just focused on batches.

BATCH-AND-QUEUE

Producing more than one piece of a product and then moving those items forward to the next operation before they are all actually needed there. It is rather a conventional industrial process and is avoided by TPS so as to avoid large inventories of unwanted products waiting in a queue. It is also called "Batch-and-Push." TPS contrasts with this with Continuous Flow / Pull Methodology.

BENCHMARKING

It is the procedure of measuring products, servings, and practices against those of leading organizations/entities.

It concentrates on best practices and methods of world class leaders and compares key performance practices and metrics with other organizations in similar niches or relevant work, establishing standard criteria for improvements based on what other successful organizations have been able to accomplish.

It is an upgrading process by virtue of which an organization compares its performance against best-in-class organizations, investigates how those companies or organizations achieved their high performance levels, and uses the information to improve their performance.

The subjects that can be bench marked include the following:

1. **Strategies**

2. **Products**

3. **Programs**

4. **Processes**

5. **Procedures**

6. **Services**

7. **Operations**

A SWOT (Strength, Weaknesses, Opportunities and Threats) Analysis can be used in the Benchmarking process.

BEST-IN-CLASS

A best-known example of performance in a particular field/area/operation/product. It is defined both in terms of the class and the performance based on specific criteria.

BREAKTHROUGH OBJECTIVES

The objectives that are beyond the norms of both the organization and the industry standards.

BROWNFIELD

An existing and operating production facility that is set up for mass-production manufacturing and management methods that cater to mass-production.

BOTTLENECK

A process in any part of the organization that limits the capacity of the whole process.

BUILD-TO-ORDER

This differs from repetitive manufacturing. It focuses on designing, building, and delivering a service or a product based on a customer request specific to the customer. The Pull Method used by TPS is an important model of Build-To-Order.

C

CAPACITY CONSTRAINT RESOURCES (CCR)

A situation when a series of non-bottlenecks, based on the sequence in which they perform their jobs can act as a limitation or constraint.

CATCH BALL

A procedure used in Hoshin Planning to communicate vertically for developing consensus on the "means" that will be applied to attain each "breakthrough objective".

Involves planning between managers and their staff during which data, ideas, and analysis are thrown like a ball-back, forth, up, down, horizontally across the company. This opens a productive dialogue throughout the company.

See HOSHIN KANRI

CELLULAR MANUFACTURING

The analogy is credited to how cells operate in living systems. An alignment of procedures and equipment in correct process sequence, where operators work within the cell and materials are presented to them from outside of the cell. This is a conventional form of management and is contrary to TPS's Pull system as cellular manufacturing does not take into account waste elimination or process flow.

CHAKU-CHAKU LINE

A system of performing a single-piece flow, where the operator moves form machine to machine, taking the part from one machine and loading it into the next. It is a production line where the only human activity is to 'Chaku' or 'Load' the machines. The machines throw out the finished parts automatically using Hanedashi, so that the operator/s do not have to hang around.

See LOAD-LOAD and HANEDASHI

CHANGE AGENT

A Change Agent shifts the paradigm from micro-management systems to dynamic macro-management leadership systems whereby the organization sees itself as part of an organic need within the customer niche and not just a myopic entity.

An individual who will lead the company and its staff from the traditional mentality to becoming a Lean Organization. It is a prerequisite that this individual leads the cultural change in an organization via the creation of a fresh paradigm so that the old paradigm is simultaneously rendered obsolete.

For instance the idea of the Change Agent is to help cause the transformation from Current State (traditional processing, e.g. push, batch and queue) to Future State (Lean Management, PULL).

CHANGE MANAGEMENT

The methodology of implementing of a cultural change in an organization via:

1. Planning

2. Preparing

3. Educating

4. Resource Allocating

CHANGEOVER

The time from when the last good piece of a product comes off of a machine or process until the first good piece of the next product is made.

Changeover time includes the following:

1. Set-up

2. Warm up

3. Trial run

4. Adjustment

5. First piece inspection

6. **Adjustment:** first-item inspection, materials/equipment tweaking, trial runs.

7. **Preparation:** getting ready to make the change)

8. **Positioning:** locate the materials in the correct location for use for the task/step

9. **Replacement:** removing and replacing files, program, etc.

CONCURRENT ENGINEERING

For Concurrent Engineering to function, it is a perquisite that up-front planning and dedicated resources are allocated in the initial stages of development.

It involves synergistic designing of a product or a service and its production process, the supporting information flow, and its delivery mechanism all at the same time.

The benefits include:

1. **Lower overall development cost**

2. **Lower product or service unit cost**

3. **Shorter development time from concept to market**

4. **A higher product quality**

CONSTRAINT

Any limitation in a system that acts as an impediment in the organization's ability to achieve higher performance.

See BOTTLENECK

CONTINUOUS FLOW

Part of the TPS methodology. Every step in the process whether administrative or shop-floor, makes or completes only the one piece that the next step or process needs, and the batch size is one – single-piece flow or one-piece flow based on PULL Methodology. Continuous Flow is the opposite of batch-and-queue.

See BATCH-AND-QUEUE, PULL

CONTINUOUS IMPROVEMENT

Referred to as Kaizen in TPS. It is a culture of zero tolerance to waste and the relentless pursuit of waste elimination by continually creating a better workplace, better products, and greater value to safety, society and the environment.

Continuous Improvement is a practical methodology that demonstrates the concept that a large number of small improvements in processes are easier to implement than major improvements and have a large cumulative effect in the long run.

As the name implies, the process is never perfect. It is inherent within the TPS system and is based on the premise that even the improvement can be improved.

It is to inculcate the best-practice of making many small improvements every day and improve overall efficiency in smaller increments as a habit.

See KAIZEN

CONTROL CHART

A statistical problem solving tool that denotes control of a process within established set ranges.

CONTROL ELEMENT

Any specific process variable that must be controlled within a set established range. The measurement of a control element indicates whether the process is operating under stable conditions or not.

COST OF POOR QUALITY

Implicit or explicit costs associated with supplying a poor quality product.

Categories include:

1. **Internal Failure Costs**

2. **External Failure Costs**

COST OF QUALITY

Implicit or explicit costs associated with supplying a quality product.

Categories include:

1. **Prevention**

2. **Appraisal**

3. **Failure**

COUNTERCLOCKWISE FLOW

A fundamental principle of Lean Manufacturing is that the flow of material and the motion of people should be from right to left, or counterclockwise.

The premise of this method came from the design of lathes and machine tools with the chucks on the left side, hence making it ergonomic for right-handed people to load from right to left.

COUNTER MEASURES

Any actions taken to bring less than expected results of a process back up to targeted goals.

COVARIANCE

The synergistic impact of one variable upon others in the same group.

CYCLE TIME

The time it takes to do one complete repetition of any particular task/step is referred to as Cycle Time. Cycle time can be categorized into:

1. **Manual cycle time**

2. **Machine cycle time**

3. **Auto cycle time**

It is commonly referred to as "touch time" or "hands-on time".

If cycle time for every step in an operation, within a complete process can be reduced to equal Takt Time, the service/product can be made in a Single-Piece Flow.

See TAKT TIME

D

DASHBOARD

Dashboards provide a readily available quick summary of process and/or product performance.

It is a visual tool used for collecting and reporting data about vital customer requirements and performance indices.

DAYS SUPPLY OF INVENTORY (DSI)

The days sales of inventory value, or DSI, is a financial measure of an organizations performance that gives investors an idea of how long it takes a company to turn its inventory (including goods that are a work in progress, if applicable) into actual sales.

By and large, a lower (shorter) DSI is favoured, but it is important to note that the average DSI varies from one industry to another due to various variables.

Here is how the DSI is calculated:

$$\text{Days Sales of Inventory} = \left(\frac{\text{Inventory}}{\text{Cost of Sales}} \right) \times 365$$

See INVENTORY TURNOVER

DEPENDENT EVENTS

Events that follow only after a preceding event.

DESIGNED FOR MANUFACTURING AND ASSEMBLY (DFMA)

A design process for improving of the manufacturing and assembly processes focused on:

1. **Cost**

2. **Quality**

3. **Safety**

DESIGN OF EXPERIMENT (DOE)

Also known as Experimental Design.

A DOE is the planning required for conducting experiments and evaluating the results.

The term experiment is defined as the systematic modus operandi carried out under controlled conditions in order to find out an "unknown effect", to test or establish a hypothesis, or to experimentally verify a "known effect".

E

80/20 PRINCIPLE

Also known as:

- **Pareto Principle**

- **Principle of Factor Sparsity**

- **Law of the Vital Few**

A rule of thumb that states that 80% of outcomes can be attributed to 20% of the causes for any given situation.

In business, the 80-20 principle is used to assist managers identify problems and establish which operating factors are most important and should receive the most attention based on an efficient use of resources. Resources should be allocated to concentrating on the input factors that have the most effect on a company's final results.

EIGHT WASTES – ACTIVITY

The 8 types of waste that describe all wasteful activity in a work environment are:

1) Overproduction
2) Transportation
3) Excess Motion

4) Waiting
5) Over-processing
6) Inventory
7) Errors/Defects
8) Underutilized People

Elimination of the above leads to enhanced results.

ELEMENTS OF WORK

The elements of work are as follows:

1. **Value-added work**

2. **Non value-added work**

3. **Waste**

By understanding the elements of work in detail, we focus on problem solving as a key component of Lean Management.

ERROR-PROOFING

Also known as Mistake-Proofing.

A process of TPS that deals with both the work/product and the processes to detect errors before they become defects.

See POKA-YOKE

EXTERNAL SET-UP

All set-up tasks that can be performed while the equipment is working, for instance:

1. **Collecting tools**

2. **The next piece of material**

3. **Preparing or fixtures**

Moving set-up actions from internal to external, so as to reduce down-time is a central activity of set-up reduction and SMED.

See SMED

EVAPORATING CLOUDS

It is used in Conflict Resolution. A problem solving methodology used in THEORY OF CONSTRAINTS.

See THEORY OF CONSTRAINTS

EVERY PART EVERY (EPE)

Evaluated in terms of time (hours, days, weeks, months, and so on) "Every Part Every X" indicates the level of flexibility to produce whatever the customer needs.

For example, Every Part Every day would indicate that changeovers for all products required can be executed each day and the products can be supplied to the client.

F

FAILURE MODES AND EFFECTS ANALYSIS (FMEA)

The goal is to identify possible failures and implement corrective actions in order to prevent failures. A structured approach to determining the importance as per priority, of potential failures and for identifying the sources of each potential failure, such that a solution oriented response can be set.

FIRST IN FIRST OUT (FIFO)

A system of keeping track of the order in which information or materials need to be processed. The goal of FIFO is to prevent earlier orders from being delayed unfairly in favor of new orders.

FIVE S

See Chapter on 5S SYSTEM

FIVE WHY's

A very elementary but effective method of analyzing and solving problems by asking 'why?' five times (or as many times as needed) to get to the root cause of the problem. There can be more than one root cause, and in an organizational setting, usually a team would carry out a root cause analysis of a problem. There is no special technique involved for this.

FLOW

It's also known as "one-piece flow" and "make one, move one".

Each processing step finishes its work just before the next process needs the product, and the transfer batch is one. In its highest form, continuous flow means that items are processed and moved directly to the next process one piece at a time.

FLOW CHART

A trouble-solving tool that maps out the steps in a process visually. The flow (or deficiency thereof) becomes evident and the wastes and redundancies are identified.

FLOW KAIZEN

A type of Kaizen Event that looks at improving the entire value stream. It's a Radical Improvement, usually applied only once within a value stream.

See KAIKAKU

FLOW PRODUCTION

It is a method of doing things in small quantities in sequential steps, rather than in large batches or lots or mass processing. Product (or service) moves (flows) from process to process in the smallest, quickest possible increment (one piece). Only acceptable quality products or services are accepted by the downstream customer so as to negate the cumulative effect of a defect any further. It's an integral part of TPS.

See ONE-PIECE FLOW

FUNCTIONAL LAYOUT

The best practice of grouping activities/functions or machines by the type/s of operation they perform. For example, service request-entry and copiers and shredders. It's the opposite of Cells.

See CELLS

G

GEMBA

Japanese: 現場

English: actual place" or "the real place", or "the place where you work to create value".

Within each company, Gemba can be at a different place depending on the type of industry.

GEMBA PRODUCTION SYSTEM

A manufacturing operations transformation strategy based on the TPS.

GEMBUTSU

Japanese for 'actual thing' or 'actual product'.

The tools, materials, machines, parts, and fixtures that are the focus of any Kaizen activity.

GENCHI GENBUTSU

Japanese: 現地現物

English: Go and see for yourself

Literally it means to "Go see; go to the real place and see what is actually happening". Go and see the problem. On Site, With the Actual Things.

The principle is focused on the premise that practical experience is valued over only theoretical knowledge. Hence you must see the problem to know the problem and hence find a solution.

GENJITSU

Japanese: 幻術

English: 'the facts' or 'the reality'

The actual facts or the reality of what is happening on the shop floor and/or the administration.

Gembutsu is a Japanese word meaning "real thing" and it is a component of the so-called "three reals".

The Japanese approach to problem solving is that when there is a problem somewhere, one should be as near to it as possible before offering a resolution.

While observing the actual process at the actual place, the problem solver is able to obtain actual data.

This effort will allow for a decision to be based on facts, instead of relying on second hand information gathered by others.

Practically this results in short office meetings, with the substance of the inspection being completed on the shop floor.

The 3 reals are a fundamental element of Kaizen and are as follows:

1. **The actual place of work, shop floor or Gemba**

2. **The actual product or Gembutsu**

3. **The real facts and data or Gujitsu**

GREENFIELD

A new facility in which Lean Management principles are designed into processing/manufacturing and management systems right from the beginning.

H

HANSEI

Japanese: 反省

English: Self-reflection

It is one of the concepts of Japanese culture. Han (反) means "change", "to turn something over", "to see something from a different perspective", and Sei (省) means "to review", "to examine yourself". The typical translation of the whole word Hansei is usually "introspection" or "reflection".

HANEDASHI

Japanese: ハネ出し

English: labor-saving device on a production line

These are auto-eject devices that unload the part from the machine once the cycle is complete. This allows the operators to go from one machine to the next without waiting, picking up and loading parts, hence saving the operators time. Hanedashi is a key component of CHAKU-CHAKU lines.

See CHAKU-CHAKU

HEIJUNKA

Japanese: 平準化

English: Leveling, Production Smoothing

Heijunka is a pre-requisite for Just-In-Time delivery. Simply to maintain total production volume as constant as possible.

It is the overall leveling, in the production schedule, of the volume and variety of items produced in a given time period.

See LEVELING and PRODUCTION SMOOTHING

HORIZONTAL HANDLING

Horizontal handling is when projects are assigned to a person in such a way that the focus is on maximizing a certain skill set or use of certain type of equipment. The horizontal handling does not interfere with flow.

HOSHIN

Japanese: 封神演義

English: Setting a direction or setting an objective

It is a methodology for setting strategic direction for goals (with targets) and the means for achieving them in order to address business priorities to move the company to a fresh level of high performance. It involves a PDCA (Plan-Do-Check-Act) Cycle.

HOSHIN KANRI

Literally translated from Japanese, the meaning of the word Hoshin in English is "setting a direction or setting an objective." Kanri translates as "management." Put together the meaning is "the management of objectives."

It is focused methodology of policy deployment and strategic decision-making that aligns the organization on a few but vital "breakthrough" advancements.

The objectives and means to achieve the objectives are synergically cascaded down through the entire system using a series of linked matrices.

The methodology is self-correcting and encourages organizational learning and continuous improvement of the planning process itself (PDCA).

It is the selection of:

1. **Goals**

2. **Projects to achieve the goals**

3. **Designation of people and resources for project completion**

4. **Establishment of project metrics**

5. **Strategic policy deployment**

6. **A powerful strategic planning system**

It was developed in Japan in the 1960's and is also known as Policy Management or Policy Deployment, or Hoshin Planning.

In Hoshin Kanri, organizational leadership identifies critical (3-5) priority breakthrough objectives or goals and engages all other goals or projects to achieving those objectives. Then a process called CATCH BALL is used to assure that these objectives are SMART Goals.

Further it's crucial that the that resources for achieving the objectives are made available. This catch ball goes on back and forth between different levels of the company until there is alignment and agreement that the breakthrough goals are not out of focus. It has been to a ship in a storm going in the right direction or the precision of a shining needle.

See CATCH BALL, SMART GOALS

HOSHIN PLANNING

Also known as Management by Policy or, alternatively, Strategy Deployment. A process by which goals are established and actions are created to ensure progress toward those goals. It keeps activities at all levels of a business aligned with its overarching strategic plans. Hoshin Planning characteristically begins with the "Visioning Process", which deals with the key questions:

1. **Where do you want to be in the future?**

2. **How do you want to get there?**

3. **When do you want to achieve your goal?**

4. **Who will be involved in achieving the goals?**

Finally it systematically explores the what's, when's, who's and how's throughout the entire company.

I

IJO-KANRI

See ABNORMALITY MANAGEMENT

INFORMATION MANAGEMENT TASK

It is the task of taking a specific product, from order-taking, through detailed scheduling, onto delivery.

INFORMATIVE INSPECTION A

It is a form of inspection used to determine non-conforming product.

INTELLIGENT AUTOMATION

See AUTONOMATION

INTERNAL SET-UP

It is a set-up of tasks that can only be done when the machine is stopped. Examples include changing the fixture, changing the tools, or making adjustments.

INVENTORY

A major cost factor for most businesses is their inventory that includes:

1. **All raw materials**

2. **Purchased parts**

3. **Work-in-process components**

4. **Finished products that are not yet provided or sold to a customer**

INVENTORY TURNOVER

It refers to the number of times that inventory is sold or used over the course of a particular time period such as a quarter or a year.

It is an important metric for businesses, especially retailers of physical goods, the inventory turnover ratio measures a company's efficiency in terms of management, inventory and generation of sales. As with a typical turnover ratio, inventory turnover calculates the amount of inventory that is sold over a given period of time.

A simple formula for the inventory turnover ratio is as follows:

Cost of Goods Sold / Average Inventory

Or

Sales / Inventory

General, the higher inventory turnover ratio, the better it is for the company's performance, as the score indicates a greater generation of sales. However, a smaller inventory and the same amount of sales will also result in a high inventory turnover. In some cases, if the demand for a product outweighs the inventory on hand, a company will see a loss in sales despite the high turnover ratio, thus confirming the importance of contextualizing these figures by comparing them against those of industry niche market standards and competitors.

J

JIDOKA

Japanese: 自働化

English: Autonomation - automation with human intelligence

Automatically stopping a process when a defective product is detected.

Automatically stopping abnormalities and immediately notifying the worker.

The idea is to build in quality by preventing any error from going to the next step or process. Exceptions are managed in real time. Examples include Andon and Poka Yoke - also known as "autonomation with a human touch." It is one of the two main pillars of TPS.

See AUTONOMATION, ANDON, POKA YOKE

JISHUKEN

Japanese: 自主研

English: Self Study or "Autonomous study groups"

The origin of Jishuken comes from "Kanban houshiki bukachou jishu kenkyuukai" or "かんばん方式部課長自主研究会" in the original Japanese. Which translates as "Kanban system department and section manager autonomous study groups". This was shortened to "Jishuken", which is "self study". Jishuken is often called "autonomous study groups" in English. It is a management driven Kaizen activity where members identify areas in need of continuous improvement and spread information through the organization to stimulate Kaizen activity.

FRESH EYES

An important concept of Lean Management based on Observation-Based Safety.

JUDGMENT INSPECTION

A form of inspection used to find out non-conforming products.

See INSPECTION OR INFORMATIVE INSPECTION

JUST-IN-TIME (JIT)

Japanese: ジャストインタイム

Just-In-Time is one of the two main pillars of TPS.

A process methodology, to make what the customer needs, when the customer needs it, in the quantity the customer needs, using minimal resources of manpower, material, and machinery - No More, No Less.

The three elements to making Just-in-Time possible are Takt Time, Flow production, and the Pull system, as well as Standard Work. The opposite of Just-In-Time is "Just-In-Case" — avoid this temptation.

JIT requires:

1. **Waste elimination**

2. **Process simplification**

3. **Set-up and batch-size reduction**

4. **Parallel (rather than sequential) processing**

5. **Layout redesign**

Just-In-Time approaches Just-On-Time when upstream activities occur minutes or seconds before down-stream activities, so that single-piece flow is achieved.

K

KAI-AKU

Japanese: 改悪

English: Change for the worse

It's the opposite of Kaizen. Change for the worse or bad change.

KAIKAKU

Japanese: 無き改革

English: Radical Change, Reform, Innovation

It is a radical improvements or reform that affects the future value stream. Often these are changes in business best-practices of business systems.

The principals of Kaikaku can be summarized as:

1. Strive to amaze your customers, both internal and external; ask yourself "What would an ideal customer experience be?" and look for ways to make maximum contribution to that ideal state

2. Develop a creative dissatisfaction mindset; ask yourself "What would an ideal

process or workshop look like?" and search for opportunities to make radical improvements

3. Look for opportunities to do much more with much less; apply the 80/20 Principle to everything (SEE 80/20 PRINCIPLE)

4. See problems as opportunities to make things radically better and to hone your winning skills for creative problem solving

5. Challenge assumptions and the status quo; recognize that the current practice may entrap people in old ways of seeing and thinking

6. Take different perceptual positions and look at the current practice with new eyes; ask "Why and What If?" questions

7. Know how to sell your radical ideas to other stakeholders and how to overcome resistance to change.

8. Brainstorm creative solutions with your group; go wild; think outside the box; look for synergies

9. Think positively and act promptly by starting to improving things and learn as you go

10. Follow the radical improvement action (Kaikaku) with continuous small improvements (Kaizen)

Here are the 10 Commandments of Kaikaku by Hiroyuki Hirano as compiled by Norman Bodek:

1. "Throw out the traditional concept of manufacturing methods."

2. "Think of how the new method will work; not how it won't work.

3. "Don't accept excuses. Totally deny the status quo."

4. "Don't seek perfection. A 50% implementation rate is fine as long as it is done on the spot."

5. "Correct mistakes the moment they are found."

6. "Don't spend money on Kaikaku."

7. "Problems give you a chance to use your brains."

8. "Ask 'Why' five times."

9. "Ten person's ideas are better than one person's knowledge."

10. "Kaikaku knows no limits."

KAIZEN

Japanese: 改善

English: Continuous Improvement

The Japanese word for 'Continuous Iimprovement' or 'change for the 'better'.

In 1986, Kaizen was originally introduced to the West by Masaaki Imai in his book Kaizen: The Key to Japan's Competitive Success. Today kaizen is recognized worldwide as an important pillar of an organization's long-term competitive strategy. It forms the cornerstone of the TPS.

Guiding principles of Kaizen are:

1. **Good processes bring good results**

2. **Go see for yourself to grasp the current situation**

3. **Speak with data, manage by facts**

4. Take action to contain and correct root causes of problems

5. Work as a team

6. **Kaizen is everybody's business**

Kaizen can also be a continual improvement in personal life, home life, social life, and working life.

In the workplace, Kaizen means continuing improvement involving everyone regardless of the job description.

It is an operational philosophy of:

1. **Continuous cost reduction**

2. **Reduced quality problems**

3. **Delivery time reduction through rapid implementation of process flow**

4. **Team-based improvement activity**

Kaizen involves much more than improvement in basic processes as it represents a philosophy within which an company at large, and the individual staff, undertake continual improvements of all aspects of organizational development.

Kaizen is a process of incremental continuous improvement in which instances of waste (Muda) are eliminated one-by-one at minimal cost. It is performed by all employees rather than by just specialists.

The basis aspect for a successful Kaizen is:

1. **Going to the worksite (Gemba)**

2. **Working with the actual product or process**

3. **Getting the facts**

As part of the TPS philosophy, anyone in the company can set-up a Kaizen and load it on the companies enterprise management software for review by the management. If the Kaizen is not reflected upon by the management within a short period, it becomes activated and applied automatically, hence the management is forced to suggest reasons for or against the Kaizen in a proactive manner.

KANBAN

Japanese: 看板, also かんばん

English: Sign, Index Card

Kanbans are normally a card or other visual method of triggering the Pull System based on actual usage of material. It is a central factor of a Just in Time system.

Kanbans are fixed to the actual work/item/product, at the point of use.

Kanbans are cards that have information about the parts that include:

1. **Name**

2. **Part number**

3. **Quantity**

4. **Source**

5. **Destination**

However, carts, boxes, and electronic signals are also used as Kanbans.

KATA

Japanese: 型 or 形

English: The form and order of doing things

Kata is a martial arts term meaning motion or form. In the Japanese business language Kata means the "correct way". Mannerisms such as the art of bowing, exchanging name cards, the importance of an apology, and the Japanese obsession with high quality, cleanliness and waste reduction are all deeply rooted in the cultural value system of Japan.

A company's Kata can be considered as it's consistent role modelling, teaching, facilitating, implementing via practical application.

Toyota Kata is split into two fields:

- **Improvement Kata**

- **Coaching Kata**

Kata instructs the mastery of:

- **Continuous improvement**

- **Adaptiveness**

- **Innovation**

L

LAST IN FIRST OUT (LIFO)

The outcome of a typical material or information flow system without FIFO, resulting in earlier orders being perpetually delayed by new orders arriving on top of them.

See FIFO

LEAD-TIME

The total time a customer has to wait to receive a product or service after placing the order. When a scheduling and production system is moving at or below capacity, Lead Time and Throughput Time are the same. When demand surpasses the capacity of a system, there is additional waiting time and Lead Time exceeds Throughput Time.

See THROUGHPUT TIME

LEAN

Lean is simply a thought process or approach, not a tool, used to look at your business whether it manufacturing industry or any other activity where you have a supplier and a customer.

Based on the Toyota Production System (TPS), the term "Lean" was coined by James P. Womack and Daniel T. Jones in their 1996 classic, Lean Thinking.

The main ideas within Lean are identifying 'waste' from the customer perspective and then determining how to eliminate it.

Waste is defined as the activity or activities that a customer would not want to "pay" for and/or that add no value to the product or service from the customer's point of view.

Once waste has been identified in the Current State, a plan (See PDCA) is formulated to reach the Future State in an effective manner that encompasses the entire system.

LEAN MANUFACTURING

A production practice characterized by the endless pursuit of waste elimination. A manufacturer that is Lean uses the minimum amount of manpower, materials, finance, machines, spaces etc. for completion of the job on schedule.

LEAN ENTERPRISE

A Lean Enterprise is a company that is engaged in the endless pursuit of waste elimination. A Lean Enterprise has a culture that does not tolerate any kind of waste.

LEAN TRANSFORMATION

Creating a culture that is intolerant to waste in all of its forms. A successful Lean Transformation should result in the creation of a Lean Enterprise, that is engaged in the endless pursuit of waste elimination.

LEVELING

Leveling is the basic idea of a Gemba Production System. It involves smoothing out the production schedule by averaging out both the volume and mix of products.

Production leveling allows a consistent workflow, hence reducing the fluctuation of customer demand with the eventual goal of being able to produce any product in any given day.

LOAD-LOAD

A process of conducting single-piece flow, where the operator proceeds from machine to machine, while taking the part form one machine and loading it into the next. It's the same as Chaku-Chaku.

See CHAKU-CHAKU

M

MACHINE AUTOMATIC TIME

The time it takes for a machine to manufacture one unit, not including the manual time to load and unload.

MACHINE CYCLE TIME

The time it takes for a machine to manufacture one unit, including the manual time it takes to load and unload.

MANAGEMENT BY OBJECTIVES (MBO)

It's a precursor to Hoshin Planning. MBO was introduced by Peter Drucker in 1954 in his popular book, The Practice of Management.

See HOSHIN PLANNING

MANUFACTURING SUPERMARKET

Where all components are available to be withdrawn by a process.

MUDA

Japanese: 無駄 or ムダ

English: Waste

Any activity that adds cost without adding value to the product. Also defined as any human activity which absorbs resources, but creates no real value for the customer.

See NON-VALUE-ADDED, WASTE

Also see Chapter: OVERBURDEN, INCONSISTENCY, AND ELIMINATE WASTE

MURA

Japanese: 斑 or ムラ

English: Unevenness

Variations and variability in work methodology or the output of a process; an unevenness in operations.

Also see Chapter: OVERBURDEN, INCONSISTENCY, AND ELIMINATE WASTE

MURI

Japanese: 無理

English: Overburden

Overworking, overburdening of people and equipment; unreasonableness; exertion.

Also see Chapter: OVERBURDEN, INCONSISTENCY, AND ELIMINATE WASTE

MULTI-MACHINE HANDLING

A Multi-machine handling is an operation in which a machine operator is running more than one machine of a certain type.

MULTI-PROCESS HANDLING

Multi-process handling is a term used to describe an operation in which a machine operator is doing tasks for multiple processes sequentially, and this is contributing to the flow of material.

N

NAGARA

Japanese: 長良

English: while doing something

It is a TPS process that describes the accomplishment of more than one task in one motion or function. It is a system where seemingly unrelated tasks can be produced by the same worker concurrently.

NEMAWASHI

Japanese: 根回し

English: Laying the groundwork, building consensus, going around the roots, prepare a tree for transplanting.

Involves the formal and informal method of gaining consensus prior to the implementation of a Hoshin or plan (See PDCA, HOSHIN, HOSHIN KANRI). It is a dynamic consensus building methodology and requires the groundwork to involve other areas/sections/departments in discussions to seek input, information, and/or support for a proposal or change of the SOP (Standard Operating Procedure) that would affect the people involved.

NON-VALUE-ADDED WORK

Activities or actions that may or may not be necessary and do not add real value as defined by the customer; making such activities or action a type of waste. For instance: packaging, paperwork, travel, and inspection. Non-value-added activities or actions can create value if their function is to identify and eliminate waste.

O

OVERALL EQUIPMENT EFFECTIVENESS (OEE)

OEE is one of the 5 main pillars of TPS. OEE is calculated based on:

Availability x Performance x Quality

It determines how much of the time a piece of equipment is being used while it is actually 'producing' good parts at a suitable pace.

ONE-PIECE FLOW

The movement of the work/product through each step/operation as a single part, never handled in batches. One-piece flow processing is when the work/item/product is made one at a time and passed on to the next process downstream simultaneously.

The benefits of one-piece flow include the following:

1. **The quick detection of defects to prevent a large batch of defects**

2. **Short lead-times of processing**

3. **Reduced material and inventory costs**

4. **Design of workstations and equipment of the right size and design**

It reinforces near-perfect balance and coordination by creating an optimal operation.

OPERATOR CYCLE TIME

It is the time taken for a worker or machine operator to complete a sequence of operations, including loading and unloading, but does not include waiting time.

OPEN ROOM EFFECT

This is a common practice in Japanese offices that involves eliminating the walls and cubicles of an office and laying all of the desks out into one big 'open room set-up'. It saves space and improves communication between those performing related tasks and creates a sense of teamwork and synergy.

OPERATING EXPENSES

The finances required for the system to convert inventory into production.

OPERATIONS

Work or steps taken to convert material from raw materials to finished product.

P

PACEMAKER

A process point along a value stream that sets the pace for the entire stream. It can also be a device or technique used to set the pace of production and maintain Takt time optimally.

See TAKT TIME

PARADIGM SHIFT

Changing one's perception of what was believed to be acceptable and correct.

Illustration of a Paradigm Shift:

FROM:

Management makes decisions about how work should be done.
The underlying belief is that, "workers are not capable of this".

TO:

The People who do the work, are closest,
to the work, know it the best
and understand how it can be done better.

FROM:

To ensure high quality it is important to perform reviews and inspections

TO:

Reviews and inspections are part and parcel of the regular work and in themselves are really a waste of people and time, since the work should be done right the first time and that should be the focus of a proactive, living and dynamic continuously improving culture.

PARETO CHART

It is a problem solving tool in the form of a vertical bar graph presenting the bars in descending order of significance from left to right. A Pareto Chart concentrates its focus on the improvement activity and pin-points the "vital few" and not the "trivial many".

80/20 Rule comes from the Pareto Principle, stating that 20% of the items account for 80% of the activity (problems, sales, defects, mistakes, errors etc.).

See 80/20 PRINCIPLE

PDCA

PDCA stands for 'Plan-Do-Check-Act. This is a basic principle for effective problem-solving as part of Kaizen. It was developed by Walter Shewhart in the 1930's and refined by W. Edwards Deming. The PDCA simply defines the problem/waste and generating solutions/changes, implementing the solutions/changes, evaluating the solutions/changes, and acting on what has been learned – hence, the cycle starts all over again as a continuous improvement feedback loop.

PERFORMANCE MANAGEMENT

A methodology of establishing the key indicators of a business via a set of tools and approaches to:

1. **Measure**

2. **Improve**

3. **Monitor**

4. **Sustain**

PHYSICAL TRANSFORMATION TASK

It is the task of taking a specific product from raw materials to a finished merchandise in the hands of the customer.

See VALUE STREAM

PITCH

It is the amount of time needed in a production area to make one container of products ready for customer dispatch.

The formula for pitch is:

Takt Time x Pack-out Quantity = Pitch

Example:

If Takt Time (available production time per day divided by customer demand per day) is one minute and the pack-out quantity is 60, then: 1 minute x 60 pieces = pitch of 60 minutes.

Pitch, in combination with the use of a Heijunka box and material handling based on paced withdrawal, helps set the Takt image and pace of a facility or process.

The term pitch is sometimes used to indicate the span or time of a person's job.

POINT OF USE STORAGE (POUS)

Maintaining all items needed for the job at the location of use in a neat and organized manner. It is one of the goals of the 5S activity.

See Chapter 5S SYSTEM

POKA-YOKE

Japanese: ポカヨケ

English: Fail-safeing or mistake proofing or fool-proofing - to avoid (Japanese: Yokeru) inadvertent errors (Japanese: Poka)

In Poka-yoke workers are not blamed for the errors, but instead they find ways to keep errors from becoming defects.

This system rewards any worker for identifying an error and encourages proactive solution to be deployed promptly so that the error/defect does not cumulate further in the production process.

Mistake-proofing and fool-proofing devices made by designing parts, processes, or procedures such that mistakes either physically or procedurally do not occur.

A Poka-yoke is sometimes called a Baka-yoke. It's also called Error-Proofing, Mistake-Proofing or Zero Quality Control (ZQC).

They are low-cost, highly reliable devices, used in the Jidoka system, that will promptly stop processes in order to prevent the production of defective parts.

POLICY DEPLOYMENT

It is the systematic selection of goals, projects to achieve the goals, designation of people, and resources for project completion, and establishment of project metrics.

See HOSHIN KANRI

POLICY MANAGEMENT

A powerful strategic planning system developed in Japan in the 1960's. The "nervous system" of Lean Production.

It is also known as Policy Deployment and Hoshin Planning

See HOSHIN KANRI, POLICY DEPLOYMENT

PROBLEM

The discrepancies between actual and desired performance are known as problems.

Examples include the following:

1. A client has to wait too long for a service to be provided

2. Work has to be done over again

3. Work is reviewed multiple times at various stages of the process

4. Services do not match or meet the needs of the client/customer

5. Defective product

Problems are solved by making changes in the process that close these discrepancies.

See MUDA

PROCESS

It is the flow of material in time and space.

The buildup of sub-processes or operations that transform material from raw material/input to finished products.

Processes are the sequence of action steps taken to convert inputs into outcomes.

All processes have inputs, steps, and outcomes. Measurements can be made, data collected, and changes made and tested for enhancements.

Companies exist to serve their customers. Customers are served via processes. The overwhelming majority of problems that organizations experience in serving clients are caused by errors in their processes. Hence, if the company is to improve its client service, it must solve the problems in its processes as an integral part of its operation.

PROCESS CAPACITY TABLE

A chart principally used in the machining processes that compares set-up and machine load times to the available capacity.

It's also known as Table of Production Capacity by Process.

PROCESS KAIZEN

Continuous improvement through incremental improvements.

See KAIZEN

PRODUCT QUANTITY PROCESS ROUTING ANALYSIS (PQPR)

The PQ (Product Quantity) refers to Pareto analysis to determine the 80/20 rule of the top products or services that make up 80% of the volume of work.

The PR (Process Routing) refers to the Parts-Process Matrix Analysis to establish product families by grouping of products with similar process flows.

The effect of a correct PQPR results in a definition of value streams and sufficient process flow data to begin the design of one-piece flow cells.

PRODUCTION PREPARATION PROCESS (3P)

Rapidly designing processes and equipment to ensure:

a) **Capability**

b) **Built-in quality**

c) **Productivity**

d) **Takt-Flow-Pull**

The 3P minimizes resources needed such as:

a) **Capital**

b) **Tooling**

c) **Space**

d) **Inventory**

e) **Time**

PRODUCTION SMOOTHING

Maintaining total manufacturing volume as constant as possible.

See HEIJUNKA, LEVELING

PULL SYSTEM

Also referred to as Downstream Pull System. It's a vital part of TPS.

Fundamentals of Pull System:

1. The customer can be either internal or external. It's an essential part of any "Build-To-Order Strategy". Once the framework for Flow is set, the next step is to only produce what the customer needs.

2. To produce or process an item only when the customer needs it and has requested it. Also referred to as: Use One - Make One.

3. Pull means that no one upstream should produce goods or services until the customer downstream asks for it. This is in complete contrast to Push. Pull is one of the 3 main elements of Just-In-Time.

4. The Pull system enables the production of what is wanted, based on a signal of what has just been "sold".

5. The downstream process takes the product they need and 'pulls' it from the producer. This 'customer pull' is a signal to the producer that the product is sold.

6. The pull system links accurate information with the process to minimizes overproduction.

PUSH SYSTEM

It is a traditional system based on production without any real demand by either a customer or internally in-between the process.

Inevitably it creates inventory and all other 'wastes'. It is in contrast to the Pull system, the service/product is pushed into a process, irrespective of whether it is needed right now or not.

The pushed product goes into inventory, and lacking a pull signal from the customer indicating that it has been used/bought, more of the same service/product could be overproduced and put in inventory. In a Push System, creating/producing more of an item or service is based on the anticipation of its use.

A Push system attempts to predict when the item/service/material will be needed and will launch its processing in anticipation of its requirement; hence it's based on assumption as opposed to actual customer order.

Q

Q SEVEN AND THE NEW SEVEN

The Q Stands for Quality. These are the seven statistical tools, and the seven additional tools that have been the foundation of problem solving in the domain of quality.

See SEVEN TOOLS OF QUALITY CONTROL, SEVEN NEW TOOLS

QUALITY, COST, AND DELIVERY (QCD)

This is process by virtue of which the quality meets the expectation and requirements of the customer (stated and un-stated).

The QCD stands for:

- **Quality**: In most cases, this view of quality is 'conformance to specification', rather than grade of the product.

- **Cost**: It has a major role due to its close tie to profitability.

- **Delivery**: It is the ability of a company to reach their promised delivery dates.

They are the key customer satisfaction metrics that determine if a company is competitive or not.

Kaizen activity focuses on improving QCD metrics. In long term planning a QCD metrics should have zero defects as the ultimate target.

QUALITY, COST, DELIVERY – SAFETY AND MORALE (QCDSM)

It is a set of performance management measures that includes employee satisfaction in terms of safety and morale as well as customer satisfaction. Lean Management aims to:

1. **Eliminate waste**

2. **Improve QCDSM metrics**

3. **Increase profitability**

QUALITY FUNCTION DEPLOYMENT (QFD)

A tactic involving a cross-functional teams to reach an agreement on the final product specifications are based on the wishes and voice of the customer.

Basic functions:

1. It must have the commitment of the entire team.

2. It integrates the viewpoint of team members from different disciplines and ensures that their efforts are focused on resolving important trade-offs in a consistent manner against measurable performance targets for the product. It sets up these decisions through successive levels of fine tuning and detail.

3. The application of QFD eliminates costly backflows and rework as projects close in on the launch.

QUEUE TIME

It is the time an item/work/product spends in a line awaiting for the next design, request-processing, or processing step to occur.

QUICK CHANGEOVER

The skill to change tooling and fixtures quickly (usually minutes), so multiple products can be run on the same machine.

R

REAL VALUE

Quality and features of a product or service that, in the view of customers, are merit worthy and significantly add to perceived value hence worth paying for.

See VALUE-ADDED, NON-VALUE-ADDED

REENGINEERING

To rethink and redesign every process and move it closer to the customers' needs.

RESOURCE ACTIVATION

Using a resource irrespective of whether Throughput is increased.

See RESOURCE UTILIZATION

RESOURCE UTILIZATION

Using a resource in such a manner that increases Throughput.

See RESOURCE ACTIVATION

RIGHT-SIZE

Complementing and synergizing human, financial, and equipment/supply resources with Lean Management requirements.

ROOT CAUSE

The primary and fundamental underlying reason for an event or condition. The root cause is where action is required to prevent repetition of the error.

S

SENSI

Japanese: 先生

English: Teacher

Also referred to as an outside master or teacher that assists in implementing Lean best practices. In acquiring Lean Knowledge, the Sensi often is directly involved with the student in a facilitated mentorship approached.

SEQUENTIAL CHANGEOVER

Also referred to as sequential set-up.

Basic principles are:

1. As part of a flow process, when changeover times are within Takt Time, changeovers can be performed one after another.

2. A set-up team or specialist follows the operator, so that by the time the operator has completed one round of the flow line (at Takt time), it has been completely changed over to the next product.

3. Sequential changeover confirms that the lost time for each process in the line is minimized to one 'Takt' beat.

SEQUENTIAL SET-UP

See SEQUENTIAL CHANGEOVER

SET-UP REDUCTION

Reducing the time a machine or a step/process is down through changeover from the last good piece to the first good piece of the next product.

SEVEN NEW TOOLS

The 7 new tools used for problem-solving for Kaizen and Hoshin Kanri activities are:

1) **Matrix diagram**

2) **Relationship diagrams**

3) **Process decision program charts**

4) **Activity network diagrams**

5) **Radar charts**

6) **Tree diagrams**

7) **Affinity diagrams**

SEVEN TOOLS OF QUALITY CONTROL

The data gathering and analysis tools used for Kaizen activities originally by Quality Control are:

1) Check sheets

2) Cause and effect diagrams

3) Pareto diagrams

4) Histograms

5) Graphs

6) Scatter diagrams

7) Broken line graphs

SEVEN WASTES - PHYSICAL

The original enumeration of the wastes commonly found in physical production as suggested by Taiichi Ohno's are:

1. **OVERPRODUCTION:** Manufacture of products in advance or in excess of demand wastes finances, time, resources and space.

2. **WAITING:** Processes are unproductive and time is wasted when one process waits to begin while another ends. Instead of this, the flow of operations should be smooth, uninterrupted and continuous. Estimates suggest that as much as 99 percent of a product's time in manufacture is actually spent "waiting". International Journal of

Emerging Technology and Advanced Engineering Certified Journal, Volume 3, Issue 11, November 2013).

3. **TRANSPORTATION:** Unnecessary transport of materials (for example, between functional areas of facilities). Transporting a product between manufacturing processes adds no value, is expensive and can cause damage or product deterioration if left for long periods.

4. **INAPPROPRIATE PROCESSING:** Over-processing of parts due to poor tool and product design. Excessively elaborate and expensive equipment is wasteful if simpler machinery would work just as effectively.

5. **EXCESSIVE INVENTORY:** Inventories more than the absolute minimum wastes resources through costs of storage, maintenance and product deterioration.

6. **UNNECESSARY MOVEMENT:** By employees during the course of their work (looking for parts, tools, prints, help, etc.). Resources and time are wasted when workers have to bend, reach or walk distances to do their work. Workplace ergonomics assessment should be conducted to design a more efficient working environment that also incorporates eliminating occupational hazards and attention to safety.

7. **DEFECTS:** Production of defective parts and inspecting and quarantining inventory takes time and the financial impact is high.

SHIGEO SHINGO

Japanese: 新郷 重夫

The Japanese innovator and theorist of important innovations related to Industrial engineering, such as Poka-yoke, Zero Quality Control, Single Minute Exchange of Die (SMED). He is considered as one of the world's leading expert on manufacturing practices and the Toyota Production System.

SHOJINKA

Japanese: 書き込み

English: Flexible manpower line

It is a type of flexible manufacturing, where the number of workers vary to match requirements of the demand. This is perceptibly better to a static system that staffs work areas without consideration for fluctuations in production. Thus the ability to be able to reassign people to exactly where they are needed helps keep production areas from falling short. Shojinka also releases people to work on improvement projects when demand is low.

SHUSA

Japanese: 主査

English: Leader

It's the leader of the team whose responsibility is to design and engineer a new product and put it into production via actualizing the design process.

SIX SIGMA

Six Sigma is a statistical term that equates to 3.4 defects per one million opportunities.

A method and set of tools used to improve quality to less than 3.4 defects per million or better.

Typically companies/manufacturers aim to operate at around three sigma, or 67,000 defects per million.

Six Sigma can attain remarkable improvement in business performance through a precise understanding of customer requirements and the elimination of defects from existing processes, products and services. To come to grip with Six Sigma, a company must work closely with all internal disciplines in addition to external suppliers and customers.

Key aspects of Six Sigma are:

1. **Define**

2. **Measure**

3. **Analyze**

4. **Improve**

5. **Control**

SKILLS MATRIX

Every professional organisation should invest in setting up of a Skills Matrix for each department. The benefits of doing so significantly prevail over the small investment.

A skills matrix is a table that clearly and visibly illustrates the skill level held by individuals within a department. Its main aim is to assist in the understanding, awareness, development, deployment and tracking of people and their skill sets. Skills matrices should identify any gap between the skill sets that are required by the job and the skills of individual employees.

The information acquired via the skills matrix is used to create a training calendar. (See SKILL MATRIX and TRAINING CALENDAR TEMPLATES in the Flowcharts - Integrating TPS Section).

Benefits of setting up a skill matrix are as follows:

Benefits to the employee

- Increased competencies – a sense of investment into the development of the employee.

- Removing uncertainty – hence leads to decreased stress levels and increase in competencies.

- Detailed awareness of what their job involves and focus on building a need based training plan.

- Personal Development Plans (PDP) – The skills matrix is a Key Performance Indicator (KPI) of the employee.

- Employees grow from better identification and understanding of their own strengths, weaknesses, and opportunities.

- Boost morale via aiding in understanding of the value they bring to themselves and the organisation.

Benefits to the organisation

- Enables clear transparency for the managers to understand the skill strengths and weaknesses of employees.

- Capacity Building – Via showing skills shortages and increasing employee competencies companies can release real capacity into their businesses without incurring the heavy costs of recruitment and high employee turnover due to lack of training and employee dissatisfaction.

- Creates the ability to search for and fill in the need for desired skills and talents across the company.

- Management can effectively see areas of skill strength and weakness via a front page view of skills and skills gaps across an organization and can enable proficient future planning in closing the gap between required skills and actual skills.

- Drives an organisation forward via a clear and transparent view of employee skills.

Benefits to the customer

- Faster response rates and a decreased lead time.

- Increased levels of customer satisfaction via high competency of employees, and their ability to resolve queries in a timely manner.

- Quality - reduced defects and return rates and high of quality in service and/or products.

- Increased delivery times - increased employee competencies leads to efficiency and speed which can result in 'quicker to market' products and/or services.

- Customers feels valued as satisfied employees make the customers feel valued.

- Customers experience a very easy and hassle free experience with the organization.

- Customer loyalty – customers experience a high quality product and/or service hence increasing the chances of buying the product again and even advertising your products and/or services.

SMART GOALS

S - SPECIFIC

Say exactly what you want in clear, actual terms.

M - MEASURABLE

Create traceable indicators that focus on measurements. Create standards and then begin measuring and accessing based on the standards. The premise is that what gets measured gets done as it is a pragmatic standard.

A - ATTAINABLE

Goals should stretch us, yet be within reason, realistic and balanced with our priorities.

R - RELEVANT

The goal must be within the parameters of the companies vision, mission and overall objectives. It should create value in the minds of the customer.

T - TIME BOUND

If you don't have a time-line you don't have a set-goal. Create milestones and road maps to measure effectively and track your progress.

SINGLE MINUTE EXCHANGE OF DIES (SMED)

A method of a series of techniques created and developed by Shigeo Shingo for set-up reduction and quick changeovers. The long-term objective is always Zero Setup, in which changeovers are instantaneous and do not get in the way of the continuous flow process.

See SHIGEO SHINGO

STANDARDS OPERATING PROCEDURES (SOP'S)

Setting up of a **Standardized Operating Procedures (SOP's)**; a manual that incorporates the process as well as quality, environmental and safety standards. This is followed via **visuals** which break down the work process **demonstrably**. If a new staff member is introduced to the process, they should be able to follow the process simply by following the SOP's. This then forms the backbone of a sophisticated work culture.

SOP'S involve comparison with accepted norms, such as the ones set by international regulatory bodies. Examples are: Environmental Health and Safety Management Systems that includes ISO 14001 (Quality Training) and OHSAS 18001 (Occupational Health and Safety Management Systems Training).

STANDARD WORK

Standardized work is planned while focusing on human motion and creates an efficient production sequence without any waste.

Identifying specific tasks to be done the best way to get the job done in the amount of time available while ensuring the job is done right the first time, every time.

The components of standard work are:

1. **Takt Time**

2. **Work Sequence**

3. **Standard Work-in-Process**

Engaging in standard work allows for a clear and visible 'standard operation'. Divergence from standard work indicates an abnormality, which is then a prospect for improvement.

Standard Work is the most efficient and optimal synergistic combination of:

1. **Human**

2. **Machine**

3. **Material**

STANDARD IN-PROCESS STOCK

The minimum quantity of parts/items constantly available for processing on and between sub-processes.

It allocates the staff to do their job constantly in a set sequence of sub-processes, repeating the same operation.

STANDARD WORK COMBINATION SHEET (SWCS)

A document describing the sequence of production procedures allocated to a single worker performing Standard Work. It highlights the best combination of worker and machine.

STANDARD WORK SHEET (SWS)

It is a visual work instruction drawing for Standard Work.

It illustrates the:

1. **Work sequence**

2. **Takt time**

3. **Standard working process**

4. **Layout of the cell or workstation**

STANDARD WORK IN PROCESS (WIP or SWIP)

It is the minimum work-in-process needed to maintain standard work.

The Standard parts are:

1. **Parts that are completed and in the machine after auto cycle**

2. **Parts placed in the equipment with cycle times exceeding Takt time**

3. **Parts currently being worked on or handled by the operators performing standard work**

STATISTICAL FLUCTUATIONS

The types of information that cannot be precisely predicted or controlled.

STOP-THE-LINE AUTHORITY

Stop-the-line authority is a situation whereby workers are able stop the line to indicate a problem. The production line or machine will remain stopped until the supervisor, manager, engineer, maintenance personnel, support staff or the company director, has/have identified the problem and taken the necessary corrective action to get back to normal operation.

STRATEGIC PLANNING

Creating short and long-term competitive strategies using tools such as PDCA and/or SWOT Analysis to assess the current situation, develop missions and goals, and create an implementation plan to deal with the status quo in a pragmatic and SMART manner.

See PDCA, SWOT ANALYSIS, SMART

SUB-OPTIMIZATION

A situation where gains made in one activity are offset by losses in another activity or activities, and are hence inversely proportional.

SUB-PROCESSES

It is part of a process. A series of sub-operations operations when combined make a process.

SUGGESTION SYSTEM

A system by virtue of which workers are encouraged to identify wastes, safety issues, environmental concerns etc and submit ideas for improvement.

People are rewarded for suggestions resulting in cost savings. These rewards are typically shared among the production line or by the Kaizen team collectively, therefore creating a proactive environment.

SUNK COST

Any payments that have already taken place and cannot be undone. It is not prudent to make decisions based on sunk costs.

SUPERMARKET

It is a tightly managed amount of inventory within the value stream to allow for a Pull system to operate. A supermarket is usually situated at the end of a production line or the entrance of a u-shaped flow line.

SUPPLY CHAIN EXECUTION (SCE)

It is a strategy to improve stakeholder and customer value by optimization of the flow of products, services, and related information from source to customer.

SUPPLY CHAIN MANAGEMENT (SCM)

It is the operations of producing and satisfying the need for commodities and services and engages a trading partner community engaged in a synergistic and shared goal of fulfilling the requirements of the end client.

SUPPLY CHAIN PLANNING (SCP)

It is a process of Supply Chain Management. It coordinates assets to optimize the delivery of goods, services, and information from supplier to customer, while balancing supply and demand.

A Supply Chain Planning software incorporates the following:

1. **Overlays a transactional system to provide planning**

2. **Hypothetical scenario analysis capabilities**

3. Actual demand commitments

SWOT ANALYSIS

An acronym for Strengths, Weaknesses, Opportunities and Threats. This analysis sets into perspective an organization's planning criteria and can be used as a tool to analyze the market niche.

As an example the following areas can be assessed:

Strengths:

- Advantages of proposition
- Capabilities
- Competitive advantages
- USP's (unique selling points)
- Resources, Assets, People
- Experience, knowledge, data
- Financial reserves, likely returns
- Marketing - reach, distribution, awareness
- Innovative aspects
- Location and geographical
- Price, value, quality
- Accreditations, qualifications, certifications
- Processes, systems, IT, communications
- Cultural, attitudinal, behavioural
- Management cover, succession
- Philosophy and values

Weaknesses:

- Market developments
- Competitors' vulnerabilities
- Industry or lifestyle trends
- Technology development and innovation
- Global influences
- New markets, vertical, horizontal
- Niche target markets
- Geographical, export, import
- New USP's (Unique Selling Proposition)
- Tactics: e.g., surprise, major contracts
- Business and product development
- Information and research
- Partnerships, agencies, distribution
- Volumes, production, economies
- Seasonal, weather, fashion influences

Opportunities:

- Disadvantages of proposition
- Gaps in capabilities
- Lack of competitive strength
- Reputation, presence and reach
- Financials
- Own known vulnerabilities
- Timescales, deadlines and pressures
- Cash flow, start-up cash-drain
- Continuity, supply chain
- Robustness
- Effects on core activities, distraction
- Reliability of data, plan
- Predictability

- Morale, commitment, leadership
- Accreditations, etc
- Processes and systems, etc
- Management cover, succession

Threats:

- Political effects
- Legislative effects
- Environmental effects
- IT developments
- Competitor intentions - various
- Market demand
- New technologies, services, ideas
- Vital contracts and partners
- Sustaining internal capabilities
- Obstacles faced
- Insurmountable weaknesses
- Loss of key staff
- Sustainable financial backing
- Economy - home, abroad
- Seasonality, weather effects

T

TABLE OF PRODUCTION CAPACITY BY PROCESS

See PROCESS CAPACITY TABLE

TAKT TIME

Takt in German means 'pace,' 'beat,' or 'rhythm'. Takt time is one of the three elements of Just in Time (JIT).

It is the pace at which the customer is buying a particular product or service.

Takt time is:

Total net daily available "operating" time / Total daily customer demand

It is not how long it takes to perform a task. It cannot be reduced or increased except by changes in production demand or available time for work. Used in Lean Manufacturing for establishing the rhythm of the process, i.e., if the customer wants a service every three hours, the program/office should feel the pulse of producing a service every three hours.

It is the total available processing time (minus all planned activities such as breaks, check-ins, safety meetings, not available times etc.) divided by the customer's requirement/demand.

For Example:

8 Hour Shift = 480 Minutes minus

10 Minute Breaks = 460 Minutes available time

1840 Claims/Day Customer Demand/Requirements

TAKT Time = .25 minute or 15 seconds (One claim would have to be processed – at every step — every 15 seconds in order to meet the customer demand).

TARGET COSTING

A process of establishing a cost goal for a product or service in the design phase.

Target costing formula:

$$\textbf{Sales price – Target Profit = Target Cost}$$

TEBANARE

Japanese: 手離れ

English: Hands free

It aims to use low cost automation on manual machines so that people can do work that is more useful.

THEORY OF CONSTRAINTS (TOC)

A lean management theory that stresses on removal of constraints so as to increase throughput while decreasing inventory and operating expenses of the company.

THREE D'S

Working conditions or jobs that are:

1. **Dirty**

2. **Dangerous**

3. **Difficult**

THREE ELEMENTS OF DEMAND

The three drivers of customer satisfaction are:

1. **Quality**

2. **Cost**

3. **Delivery**

THREE G PRINCIPLES

The three principles are:

1. **Office floor (*Gemba*)**

2. **Actual product (*Gembutsu*)**

3. **Facts (*Genjitsu*).** The key to successful Kaizen is going to the worksite, working with the actual product/process, and getting the facts.

THREE ELEMENTS OF JUST IN TIME (JIT)

The three elements of JIT are:

1) **Takt time**

2) **Flow production**

3) **Downstream pull system**

THROUGHPUT TIME

The time taken for an item/work to proceed from concept to launch, request to delivery, or from raw materials into the hands of the customer. It includes both processing and queue time. It contrasts with Processing Time and Lead Time.

TIME-BASED STRATEGY

Moving improvement activity via focus on:

1. Time and its relation to quality

2. Cost

3. Delivery

4. Safety

5. Morale

Becoming more competitive via a reduction in:

1. Lead-time

2. Set-up time

3. Cycle time

TOYOTA PRODUCTION SYSTEM (TPS)

A system that resulted from 50+ years of Kaizen at Toyota. TPS is built on the foundations of Leveling, with the supporting pillars of Just-in-Time and Jidoka.

See also GEMBA PRODUCTION SYSTEM

TOTAL PRODUCTIVE MAINTENANCE (TPM)

It is a sequence of procedures, initially found by Nippondenso (a member of the Toyota group), to ensure that every piece of equipment in a process is always able to perform its required tasks such that processing/work is potentially never interrupted.

It seeks at maximizing equipment effectiveness and uptime throughout the entire life of the equipment. It is an integrated set of activities intended at maximizing equipment effectiveness by involving everyone in all departments at all levels, typically via small group activities.

TPM typically involves:

1. **Implementation of the 5S System**

2. **Measuring the six big losses**

3. **Prioritizing problems**

4. **Application of problem-solving with the goal of achieving Zero breakdowns**

TOTAL QUALITY MANAGEMENT (TQM)

A management approach to long–term success through customer satisfaction.

At Toyota, TQM is based on the concept of:

1. **Customer first**

2. *Kaizen* **meaning continuous improvement**

3. **Total participation which means the involvement and input of all staff in the above**

A TQM effort, involves all members of an organization in participating for the improvement of:

1. **Processes**

2. **Products**

3. **Services**

4. **Culture**

Total Quality Management has evolved via Toyota Motors to be one of the leading Lean Management methodologies in the world.

The Primary Elements of TQM are as following:

1. **Customer-focused**

2. **Total employee involvement**

3. **Process-centered**

4. **Integrated system**

5. **Strategic and systematic approach**

6. **Continual improvement**

7. **Fact-based decision making**

8. **Communications**

The above elements are understood to be so essential that many organizations define them, in some format, as a set of core values and principles on which the organization is to operate and set up the foundation of their development.

TSURUBE SYSTEM

It is also called the "Well Wheel System" as it analogous to how water is drawn out of a well using two buckets and a pulley wheel. It is often used when the work/product leaves the flow line for processing through equipment that cannot be placed into the work area. It is a method to keep product flow continuous even if there are interruptions such as outside processing or batch operations within the process at large.

TWO-BIN SYSTEM

It is an example of both visual management and the Pull system, whereby two bins or containers are used to trigger reorder of parts or materials. Each bin contains enough parts to last during the delivery lead-time. When one bin is empty, it is time to reorder the two-bin quantity and so the cycle continues.

U

UPTIME

Generally, it is expressed as a percentage; uptime is the ratio of the availability time to the actual work/production time.

It is the time a person, program, printer, copier, etc. is "available" as opposed to the time each is "expected" to be available/run for the step/task. For instance, the time a supervisor is available for signatures, the time a copier works and is available.

V

VALUE

It is a product or service's capability provided to a customer at the right time, at an appropriate cost/price, as defined by the customer.

Whatever does and or does not create value is to be specified and defined from the customer's perspective and not from the perspective of individual organizations, departments etc.

VALUE-ADDED ANALYSIS

It is an activity by virtue of which an improvement team strips the process down to its bare essential components. It involves isolation of the activities that, in the eyes of the customer, "actually add value" to the service/product. The remaining non-value-adding activities are considered as "waste", and are hence targeted for either improvement or deletion.

VALUE-ADDED WORK

These are activities that add real value to the product or service. These involve activities that are essential to ensure a product or service meets the needs of the customer.

See NON-VALUE-ADDED

VALUE STREAM

Cumulative activities, both value-added and non-value-added, required to bring a product or service from order to the hands of the customer; and a design from concept to launch, and from production to delivery is referred to as Value Stream.

VALUE STREAM MAPPING (VSM)

It is a tool used to picture the value stream of a process, department, or organization.

It shows the "Current State" and the "Future State" and maps the improvements towards a long-term "ideal state".

It is a practical tool used to:

1. **Follow** a product/information, activity path from beginning to end and draw a visual representation of every process (value and non-value) in the material and information flow charts

2. **Design** a future state map which removes waste and creates a more effective flow

3. **Finish** up with a detailed implementation plan for the future state

VERTICAL HANDLING

When tasks are allocated in such a way that the movement of the materials and processes are being progressively worked towards completion. It is in contrast to horizontal handling in which the only focus is on the output of a specific process.

VISUAL CONTROLS

It is the posting of visual signs in plain view, for all tools, parts, processing activities, and indicators of process system performance, so everyone involved can understand the status of the system at any single look.

Visual controls are tools of visual management such as:

1. **Color-coding**

2. **Charts**

3. **Andons**

4. **Schedule boards**

5. **Labels and markings on the floor**

It creates transparency and an effective work culture.

Visual controls is the displaying of the status of an activity such that every employee can see it and take appropriate action based on the display.

VISUAL MANAGEMENT

It is a situation whereby a normal state and abnormal state can be clearly and visually defined. Corrective action can be taken and any variance to standard is noticed via visual management.

W

WASTE

Everything that uses resources, but does not add real value to the product or service is referred to as waste as part of a Lean Management system.

See MUDA 8 WASTES

WELL WHEEL SYSTEM

See TSURUBE SYSTEM

WATERSPIDER

It is named after the Whirligig beetle that swims swiftly. Is a skilled and highly trained and competent individual who makes the rounds supplying parts, assisting with changeover, providing tools and materials, and any additional help needed to maintain standard operations and hence maintain the work flow.

The waterspider has a routine and knows all processes thoroughly enough to step in if required as an aid or as a relief. Toyota has made it a prerequisite role for moving on to a supervision and management position.

WORK IN PROCESS

Materials, information, people that are in-between steps or processes or activities waiting to be processed.

WORK SEQUENCE

The SOP's (Standard Operating Procedures) that need to be performed in order for the work to be accomplished. It refers to the sequence of set operations in a single process which leads a worker to produce quality goods/services efficiently and in a manner which reduces overburden and eliminates or minimizes the risk of injury or illness.

Y

YAMAZUME

Japanese: 山詰め

English: To stack up

A Yamazumi board is a bar graph characteristically showing the balance of workloads as operator cycle times. It can also be used for load planning and scheduling.

YIELD

It is the produced product (actual) related to scheduled product (planned).

YOKOTEN

Japanese: 横展

English: Across everywhere, best practice sharing, horizontal deployment

Fundamentally, it is the dissemination of information across the organization. Central to this is that it is not just the result that is shared, but also the process that led to the result in the first place.

It is a process for sharing learning laterally across an organization and also encompasses copying and improving on Kaizen ideas that work at other places.

Another Japanese phrase which is often associated with building a Yokoten culture is Kaze Toushi (風通し) which literally means "ventilation" or "wind blowing through" and is analogous to the openness or ease of communication between individual departments and with other business affiliates such as supply chain.

Yokoten has been thought of as "horizontal deployment" or "sideways expansion". Yokoten is not just about simply copying but learning from and building upon, based on the example and the specific adaptation in another given area.

Z

ZERO TOLERANCE TO WASTE

Zero tolerance to waste is an attitude of turning every employee into a quality inspector and waste elimination expert.

It is a best practice by virtue of which the staff "walk the talk" and maintain express standards for zero tolerance for errors, defects, or waste by practically demonstrating a proactive solution oriented response towards it.

FLOWCHARTS: INTEGRATING TPS

LEAN TOOLS

Copyright © 2016 Gabriel Iqbal

STANDARD WORK	**POKA-YOKE** **(MISTAKE PROOFING)**
VALUE STREAM MAPPING	**POINT OF USAGE**
ONE PIECE FLOW	**5S VISUAL MANAGEMENT**
KANBAN **DEMAND PULL**	**TPM** **TOTAL PREVENTATIVE** **MANAGEMENT** **EQUIPMENT RELIABILITY**
FMEA **FAILURE MODES AND EFFECTS** **ANALYSIS**	**SMED** **SINGLE MINUTE EXCHANGE** **OF DIE** **QUICK CHANGE OVER**

LEAN MANAGEMENT

Copyright © 2016 Gabriel Iqbal

PEOPLE	SYSTEMS
Respect	5S System
Teamwork	Kaizen (Continuous Improvement)
Consensus Building	Waste Elimination
Talent Management	Challenge
	Genchi Genbutsu (Going to the root of the problem)
	Sustainability

KAIZEN TOOLS

ONE PIECE FLOW	KANBAN (SIGNS, INDEX CARDS)
HEIJUNKA (WORK LEVELING)	VISUAL OPERATIONS
TQM TOTAL QUALITY MANAGEMENT	5S VISUAL MANAGEMENT
POKA-YOKE (MISTAKE PROOFING)	EIGHT WASTES 1) Overproduction 2) Transportation 3) Excess Motion 4) Waiting 5) Over-processing 6) Inventory 7) Errors/Defects 8) Underutilized People

SOP'S

STANDARD OPERATING PROCEDURES

TPM

TOTAL PREVENTATIVE MANAGEMENT

EQUIPMENT RELIABILITY

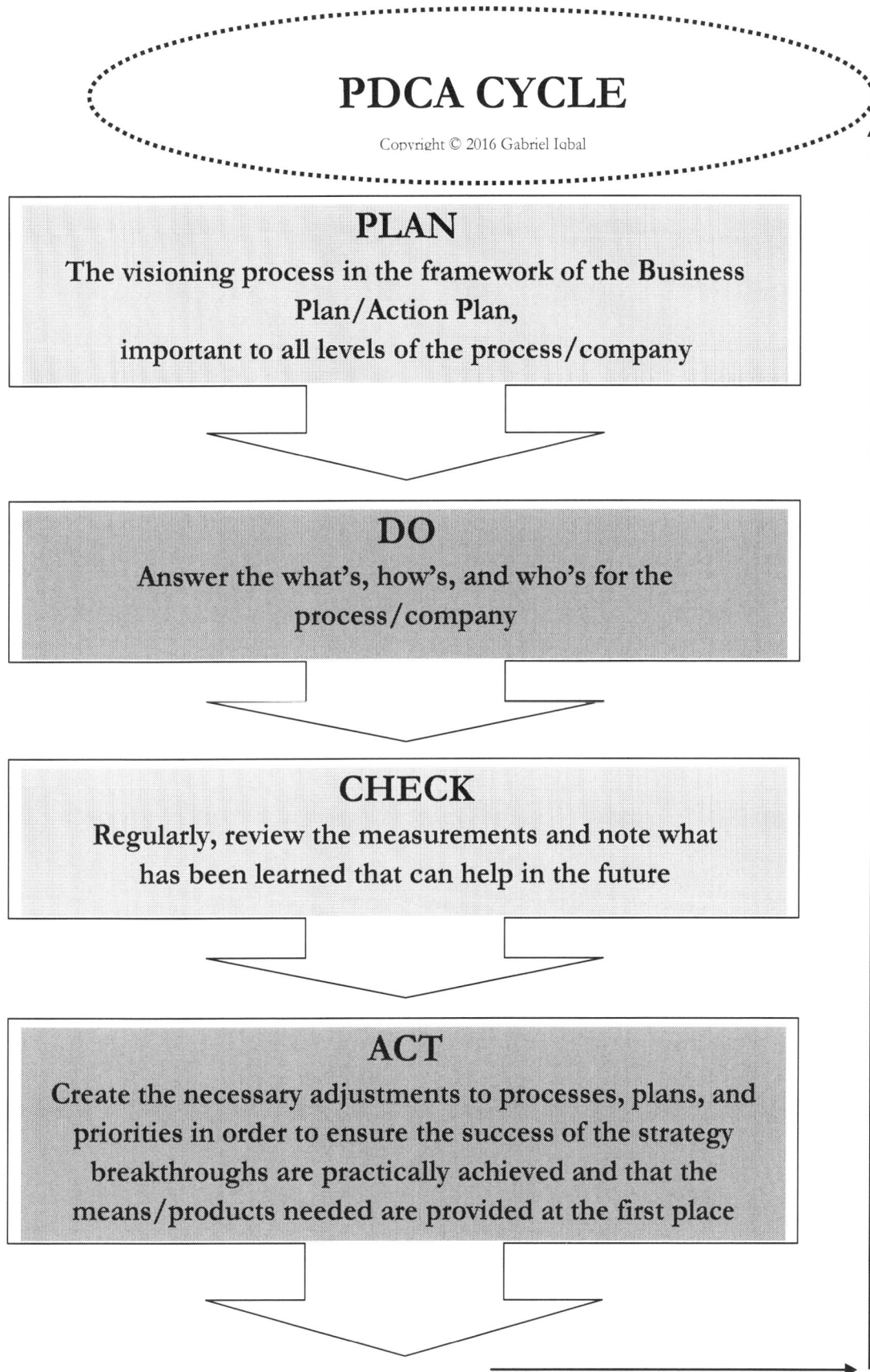

PDCA CYCLE

Copyright © 2016 Gabriel Iqbal

PLAN

The visioning process in the framework of the Business Plan/Action Plan, important to all levels of the process/company

DO

Answer the what's, how's, and who's for the process/company

CHECK

Regularly, review the measurements and note what has been learned that can help in the future

ACT

Create the necessary adjustments to processes, plans, and priorities in order to ensure the success of the strategy breakthroughs are practically achieved and that the means/products needed are provided at the first place

THE EXPERIMENTAL METHOD

Can be applied to the Kaizen and PDCA Process

(Plan-Do-Check-Act)

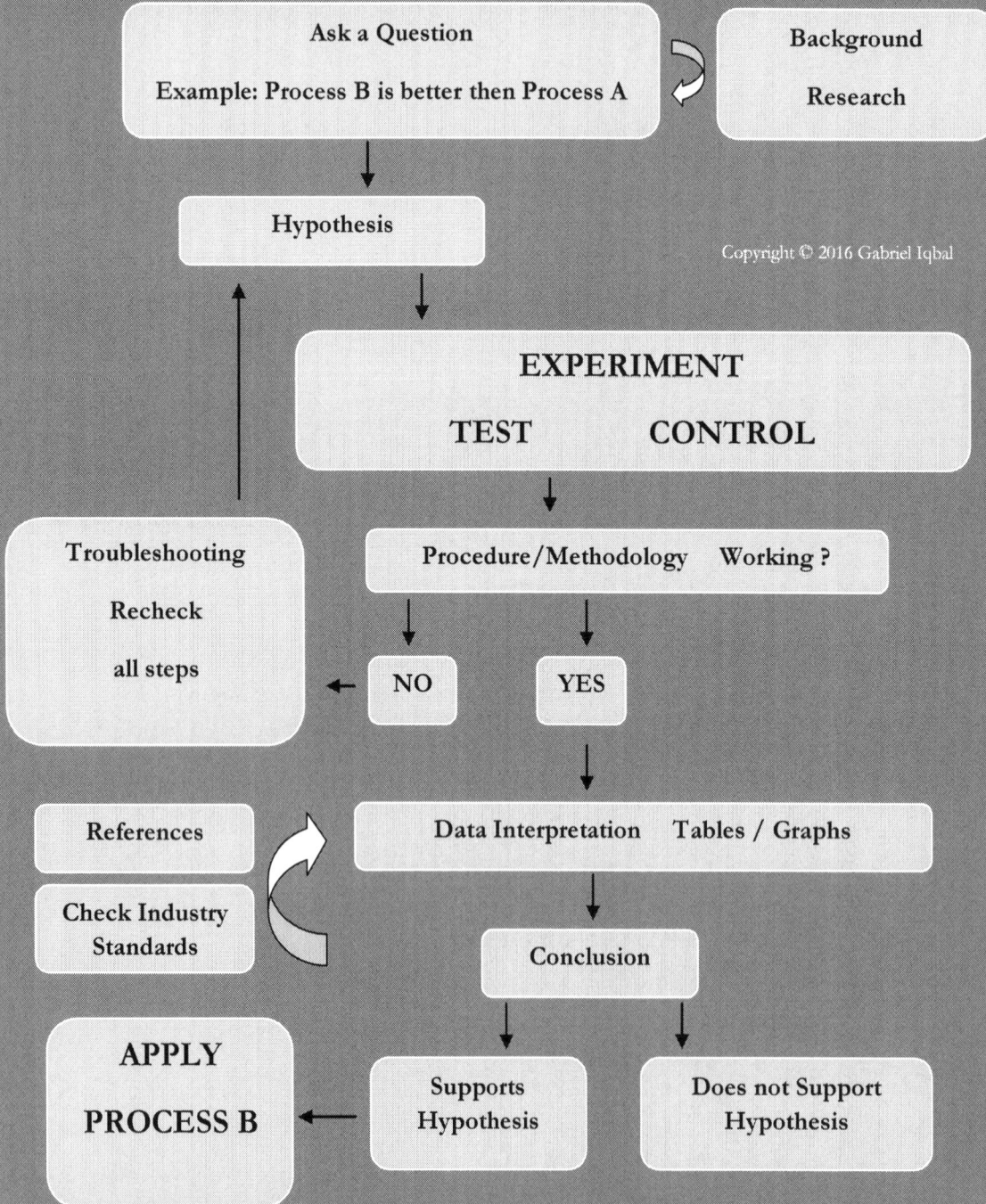

Ask a Question Example: Process B is better then Process A	Background Research

Hypothesis

Copyright © 2016 Gabriel Iqbal

EXPERIMENT

TEST   CONTROL

Procedure/Methodology   Working ?

Troubleshooting Recheck all steps

NO   YES

References

Check Industry Standards

Data Interpretation   Tables / Graphs

Conclusion

APPLY

PROCESS B

Supports Hypothesis   Does not Support Hypothesis

PULL V/S PUSH

Copyright © 2016 Gabriel Iqbal

Pulled by "Customer Demand"

P U L L

Supplier Foundry Machinery Assembly Warehouse Customer

- Material Pulled
- Required Quality
- Required Time
- Signaling:
- SIMPLE and DIRECT

- Low Inventory
- Just in Time
- Eliminates Waste

Pushed "Through Batched"

P U S H

Supplier Foundry Machining Assembly Warehouse Customer

- Traditional Manufacturing
- Unpredictable

- High Inventory
- Slow or Fast

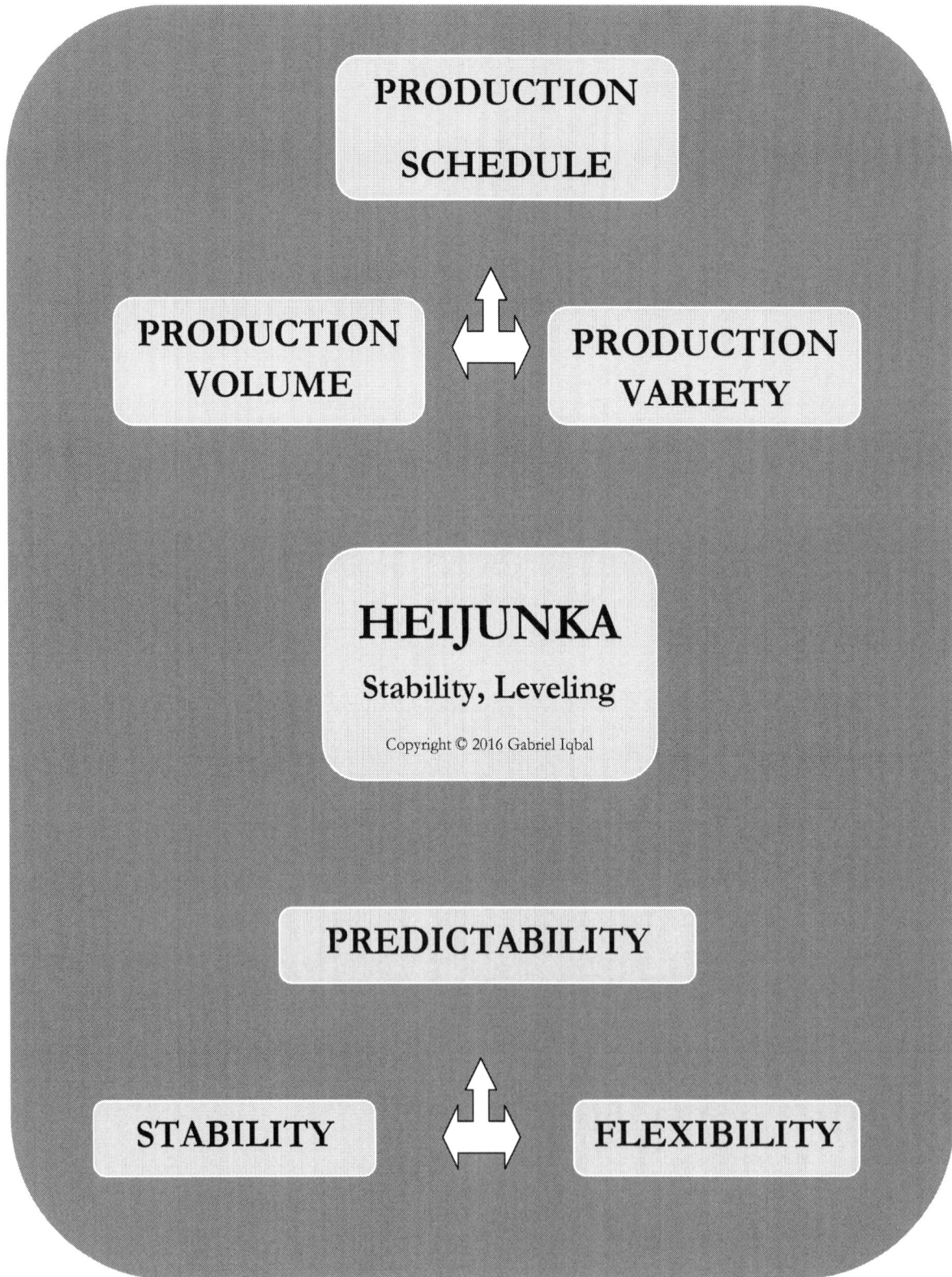

TECHNICAL SKILLS TRAINING CALENDAR TEMPLATE

S. No	Program	Dept.	Trainees	TRAINER Internal External	Dates	Month											
						1	2	3	4	5	6	7	8	9	10	11	12
1	5S System																
2	Kaizen Planning																
3	Lean Tools																
4	Pull System																
5	7 Wastes																
6	Red Tagging																
7	ISO 9001																
8	ISO 14001																
9	ISO 18001																
10	5S System																
	TOTAL																
	TOTAL COMPLETED																

Training Calendar (Technical Skills)
Copyright © 2016 Gabriel Iqbal

Planned   Conducted   TBA   X   Cancelled

Doc.Ref.No: /HR/ Date:

SKILLS MATRIX TEMPLATE

Skills Matrix Copyright © 2016 Gabriel Iqbal					
Program	**Employee Names**				
5S System					
Kaizen Planning					
Lean Tools					
Pull System					
7 Wastes					
Red Tagging					
7 Habits					
ISO 9001					
ISO 14001					
ISO 18001					
TOTAL					
TOTAL COMPLETED					
	Proficiency Level	Efficient			
		Good			
		Satisfactory			
		Not Applicable		X	

HIGH SUSTAINABILITY AND ENVIRONMENTAL STANDARDS

"Problems cannot be solved at the same
level of thinking that created them."

Albert Einstein

WASTE REDUCTION

What is unanimously true across the vehicle manufacturing industry and any major production industry, is that Toyota's manufacturing process is in itself the most effective and least waste generating process in terms of: resource, time, effort etc. Subsequently Toyota produces high quality vehicles that are known for their long lasting reliability and efficiency.

HIGH FUEL EFFICIENCY AND LOW CO2 EMISSIONS

Within their respective categories, Toyota vehicles are among the most fuel efficient and have the least amount of CO2 emissions.

HYBRID

In 1997, Toyota launched the world's first Hybrid (Gasoline/Electric) the Toyota Prius, a full hybrid electric mid-size hatchback. The United States Environmental Protection Agency and California Air Resources Board (CARB) rate the Toyota Prius as the cleanest least emissions vehicles sold in the United States. The Prius family total global sales of 5.2 million units in July 2015, represented 65.4% of the 8 million hybrids sold worldwide.

In 2011, Prius family included the Prius v, an extended hatchback wagon, and the Prius c, a subcompact hatchback. In 2012, the Prius plug-in hybrid was released.

Toyota states that lifetime CO_2 saving for the Prius is 43 percent.

The UK Government Car Service runs over 100 Priuses, the largest part of its fleet. In 2010, they listed the Prius as having the lowest CO_2 emissions among its entire fleet of cars.

Toyota has tested the wireless charging for a future Prius PHV in 2014.

ELECTRIC

Fully Electric Car: The Toyota iQ EV is a zero emission car running on 100 percent electricity.

HYDROGEN FUEL CELL

In 2015, Toyota Mirai a hydrogen fuel cell vehicle was launched, that has zero emissions and uses only Hydrogen as fuel, which is turned into water-vapour as a bi-product. Miria in Japanese means the future. Engine: Toyota Fuel Cell System, 152 bhp.

CONNECTING THE DOTS TO ACHIEVE SUSTAINABLE DEVELOPMENT

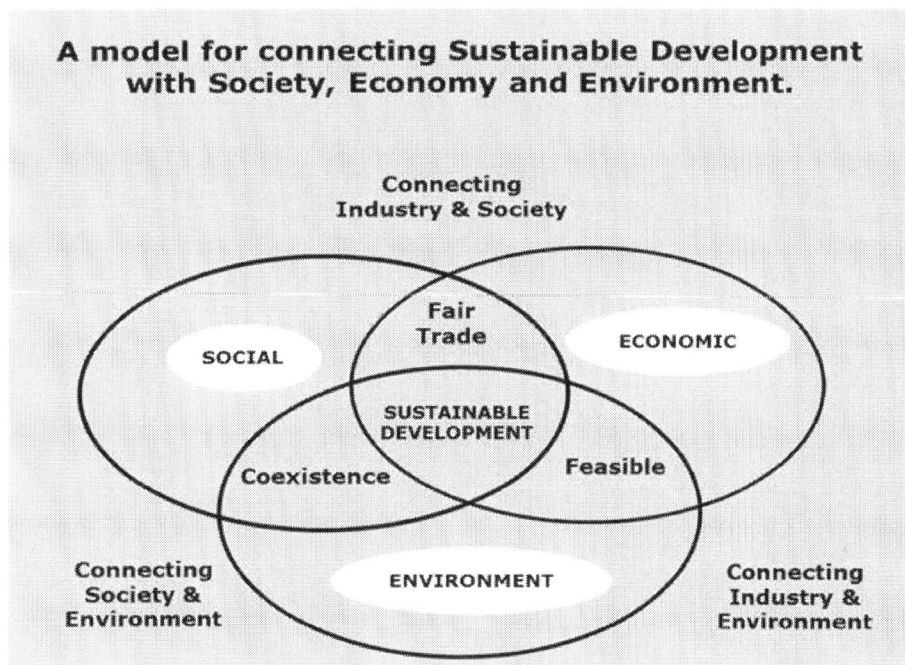

A model for connecting Sustainable Development with Society, Economy and Environment.

Connecting Industry & Society

SOCIAL

Fair Trade

ECONOMIC

SUSTAINABLE DEVELOPMENT

Coexistence

Feasible

Connecting Society & Environment

ENVIRONMENT

Connecting Industry & Environment

The above is a dynamic model that I have envisaged in my book trilogy, Heart Intelligence (Book 3) www.heartintelligencebook.com

It is a Practical Model via which I see a balanced world that can develop synergistically via harnessing the best Human Potential to create a much needed Fair, Viable and Liveable world. I can say this with all honesty that I see Lean Management and Energy Efficient technologies as a beacon of light in achieving this balance.

BIBLIOGRAPHY

Bremner, Brian, B. and C. Dawson (November 17, 2003). "Can Anything Stop Toyota?: An inside look at how it's reinventing the auto industry". Business Week.

Bodek, Norman. Kaikaku: The Power and Magic of Lean. 2004. Amazon.

Bodek, Norman and Bunji Tozawa. How to do Kaizen: A new path to innovation - Empowering everyone to be a problem solver. 2010. Amazon.

Covey, Stephen R. (1989). The 7 Habits of Highly Effective People.

Drucker, Peter. The Practice of Management. New York: Harper and Brothers. 1954.

Emiliani, B., with Stec, D., Grasso, L. and Stodder, J. (2007), Better Thinking, Better Results: Case Study and Analysis of an Enterprise-Wide Lean Transformation, second edition, The CLBM, LLC Kensington, Conn., ISBN 978-0-9722591-2-5

Goldratt , Eliyahu. Theory of Constraints, North River Press, 1990.

International Journal of Emerging Technology and Advanced Engineering
Certified Journal, Volume 3, Issue 11, November 2013) 698 Advance Industrial Approach for Waste Reduction. (Lean Manufacturing) Virender Chahal (HCTM Technical campus), Sanjeev Sharma (Associate Professor, HCTM Technical campus, Kaithal), Gulshan Chauhan (Principal, Panipat Institute of Engineering and Technology, Panipat, Kaithal. Website: www.ijetae.com (ISSN 2250-2459, ISO 9001:2008

Liker, Jeffrey (2003), The Toyota Way: 14 Management Principles from the World's Greatest Manufacturer, First edition, McGraw-Hill, ISBN 0-07-139231-9.

Magee, David (November 2007), How Toyota Became #1 - Leadership Lessons from the

World's Greatest Car Company, Portfolio Hardcover, ISBN 978-1591841791

Monden, Yasuhiro (1998), Toyota Production System, An Integrated Approach to Just-In-Time, Third edition, Norcross, GA: Engineering and Management Press, ISBN 0-412-83930-X.

Ohno, Taiichi (1995), Toyota Production System: Beyond Large-scale Production, Productivity Press Inc., ISBN 0-915299-14-3.

Ohno, Taiichi (March 1998), Toyota Production System: Beyond Large-Scale Production, Productivity Press, ISBN 978-0915299140

Shingo, Shigeo (1989) A Study of the Toyota Production System from an Industrial Engineering Viewpoint (Produce What Is Needed, When It's Needed), Productivity Press, ISBN 0-915299-17-8. (This refers to the English version; the Japanese version was published in 1981.

Spear, Steven, and Bowen, H. Kent (September 1999), "Decoding the DNA of the Toyota Production System," Harvard Business Review

Toyota Motor Corporation Sustainability Report, 2009.

Womack, James P. and Jones, Daniel T. (2003), Lean Thinking: Banish Waste and Create Wealth in Your Corporation, Revised and Updated, HarperBusiness, ISBN 0-7432-4927-5.

Womack, James P., Jones, Daniel T., and Roos, Daniel (1991), The Machine That Changed the World: The Story of Lean Production, HarperBusiness, ISBN 0-06-097417-6.

Zamprotta L., (1993), La qualité comme philosophie de la production. Interaction avec l'ergonomie et perspectives futures, Thèse de Maîtrise fr:Maîtrise ès Sciences Appliquées, TIU Press, Independence, MO, (1994), ISBN 0-89697-452-9.

PICTURE CREDITS

Samurai Warrior on Horseback (Circa 1878)
Samurai on horseback, wearing ō-yoroi armour, carrying bow (yumi) and arrows in a yebira quiver.
Author: Unknown

Painting Bamboo, Ming Dynasty (Created: 1540-1590)
Artist: Xu Wei

PUBLICATIONS BY THE AUTHOR

Books and Films

Heart Intelligence – *Book Trilogy and Film*

    Heart Intelligence: *Book 1 Powerful Self Consciousness.* 2014. Eureka Academy, Canada. Amazon.

    Heart Intelligence Film. A non-profit enterprise for public education. 2014. Eureka Academy, Canada. Available on: www.heartintelligencebook.com

    Heart Intelligence: *Book 2 Powerful Social Consciousness.* Coming soon. Eureka Academy, Canada. Amazon.

    Heart Intelligence: *Book 3 Powerful Global Consciousness.* Coming soon. Eureka Academy, Canada. Amazon.

Heart Story: *A Metamorphic Odyssey into the Heart of Human Consciousness.* 2014. Eureka Academy, Canada. Amazon.

Illustrated Encyclopedia of Science and Civilization in Islam: *The Origins and Sustainable Ethical Applications of Practical Empirical Experimental Scientific Method.* 2015. Eureka Academy, Canada. Amazon.

Rumi Soul Healer - A Transcendental Story of Ecstatic Passion and Mystical Love. 2015. Eureka Academy, Canada. Amazon.

TOYOTA Illustrated Encyclopedia of Lean Management: *An Internationally Proven Practical Step by Step Training Manual For Creating a Culture of Powerful Proactive Organizational Effectiveness, Business Success and Sustainability.* Kaizen, 5S System,

Total Quality Management, Just In Time, Pull System, Poka-Yoke, Kanban, Muda, Mura, Muri, Jidoka, Gemba... 2016. Eureka Academy, Canada. Amazon.

Environmental Research Publications

Energy Efficiency Global Challenges and Solutions. 1996. Study conducted with students from Carlton Bolling College, Bradford, UK

Fresh Water Ecology and Cultural Eutrophication. 1996. Study conducted with students from Carlton Bolling College, Bradford, UK

The Effect's of Human Impact on Biodiversity. 1996. A study conducted with students from Thomas Danby College, Leeds, UK.

Project SFFF (Save Flora and Fauna of Fujairah). 1997. Research conducted for Fujairah Municipality, UAE

How do we Deal with the Environmental Catastrophe Facing Kashmir? Model: How to Save Dal and Nageen Lake 1997

A Guide to Research the Mangrove Ecology and Environmental Degradation of Khor Kalba Mangrove. Study conducted with students from Our Own English High School, UAE. 1997

Blue Whales 1st ed. 2000. 2nd ed.2004

Human Population Dynamics: Population Growth and the Environment. 2007 Research conducted in association with students from Shanghai University.

Environmental and Social Responsibility. 2008

Vision 2050 A Dialogue on Sustainability. 2009. The Middle Eastern Perspective World Business Council on Sustainable Development List of Contributors

Sustainable Development and the Stewardship Ethic. Part 1. 2009

Sustainable Development and the Stewardship Ethic. Part 2. 2010

Energy Saving Ideas and Strategies. 2010

Environmental Management Systems Awareness Training. 2011 ISO 14001 and OHSAS 18001

Save Electricity, Save Money, Save the Earth. 2012

Effective Change Management for a Practical Environmental Campaign. 2012

Investigating the Impact of a Colony of Double Crested Cormorants on the Surrounding Ecological Niche of Hickory Island, Cootes Paradise. 2012

Biological Lessons in Coexistence. 2013

Educational Methodology Models: 2014
Reductionist, Wholistic or Sustainable Model

Leadership Development Research Publications

21st Century Leadership Paradigm Shift. 2008

Effective Management Principles. 2008

Strategic Recruitment Planning. 2008

Leadership and Perception Challenge. 2008

Powerful Well Being. 2008

Live Now. 2008

Team Building Games. 2008

Effective Management and Succession Planning. 2009

Effective Presentation Skills. 2009

Strategic Marketing Plan. 2009

5S System - Workshop. 2012

Professional Etiquette. 2012

Online publications by the author are available on:

www.eurekamakingadifference.com/research-publications

CUSTOMER REVIEW

As a token of your appreciation
we welcome you to please write a review on
Amazon

Please sign into Amazon by following link:

www.amazon.com/Gabriel-Iqbal/e/B00PTJ0OIK

Customer reviews are very import and we sincerely request a courteous review if you are inspired by the authors work and its value for the emancipation of humanity.

Thank you.

NEWSLETTER SUBSCRIPTION

Subscribe to our Free Online Newsletter:

www.eurekamakingadifference.com/newsletter

Thank you.

Confidentiality Statement:
Information about subscribers to Eureka Academy mailing lists is treated as strictly
confidential and will not be sold, shared,
or passed on to any other entity.
At any given time should you decide to unsubscribe, your details will
be erased from our records.

ORDER POSTERS and/or BOOK ORGANIZATIONAL TRAINING AND DEVELOPMENT PROGRAM

Organizational Training and Development for TOYOTA Lean Management Program designed for your team can be booked directly by contacting Eureka Academy

Large Illustrated Posters (50X70 cms)
For Organizational Training and Development are also available

Send a request on:

www.eurekamakingadifference.com/contact-us

or

email: eureka.academy@eurekamakingadifference.com

www.heartintelligencebook.com

Printed in Great Britain
by Amazon